S0-DJP-241

Angel with Crooked Feet

By
Anthony V. Sarjant, Ph.D.,
with
Gus Koernig

PublishAmerica
Baltimore

© 2006 by Anthony V. Sarjant, Ph.D., with Gus Koernig.
All rights reserved. No part of this book may be reproduced, stored in a retrieval system or transmitted in any form or by any means without the prior written permission of the publishers, except by a reviewer who may quote brief passages in a review to be printed in a newspaper, magazine or journal.

First printing

At the specific preference of the author, PublishAmerica allowed this work to remain exactly as the author intended, verbatim, without editorial input.

ISBN: 1-4241-5243-7
PUBLISHED BY PUBLISHAMERICA, LLLP
www.publishamerica.com
Baltimore

Printed in the United States of America

The big room in the old school building is filled with kids and, are they ever having a grand time! And why not? It's just a few weeks before Christmas. The kids are playing with toys, chasing one another, diving onto the floor and rolling around there, "performing" for the few adults who are there to supervise them (not much chance of that happening on this day). And all the while they're laughing in that way only children who are having a wonderful time can.

Almost all the kids are between the ages of four and fifteen. Almost all of them have parents who are incarcerated, either in the county jail or in one of the state prisons. But there is no sadness in these children, not on this day. Today they're just being kids, doing the things kids do, and loving every minute of it. The adults who've brought them together in a program for children of incarcerated parents are doing everything they can to make sure that, for at least a few hours each week, these kids don't have to even think about what life is usually like for them.

As you can imagine, with such a range in ages, the kids come in a wide variety of sizes, but even at that, one kid is noticeably larger than the others. He wears glasses and a slightly mischievous smile. There's no sadness in this kid either, and maybe that's surprising, given what he's been through. One boy describes him as "childish," even more so than the other kids. On hearing this, the big kid smiles. "Yes, I am," he laughs, "I am a bit childish, aren't I."

The big kid's name is Tony. That's me, and this is my story.

In the Beginning

I was born in an ambulance on the way to Selly Oak Hospital in Birmingham, England, on the 20th of May, 1947. I was christened that same night, because the doctors thought I wasn't going to live long. I was very frail, born with a club-foot and what doctors thought was a digestive disorder. But for the first of what would turn out to be many times, the doctors were wrong. I survived, barely. That was the good news; the bad news is that the digestive problem stemmed from a more sinister source. I had polio. The disease that would terrorize the United States in the early 1950's was actually coming under control in England in 1947 and I think I was one of the last English children to be stricken. Just my bad luck. The first of many times for that as well.

Doctors operated on my leg for the first time when I was three months old. There would be eighteen more surgeries by the time I was ten. The first was done at the Royal Orthopedic Hospital in Birmingham. I would be in hospital for as much as eight weeks at a time. My earliest memories are of lying in bed, in a room with many other small children. We all looked alike, but really we were different. The other kids had Mums and Dads who came to visit them, who brought them balloons and presents on their birthdays and at Christmastime. No one came to visit me and I was very sad and cried a lot, but I learned how to get people to notice me. When I wanted attention, or maybe out of anger, or both, I'd throw the glasses of milk and food the hospital staff brought me. Or

I would deliberately do something to hurt whoever was near me. The nurses and staff didn't like my behavior and I'm sure they didn't like me, but they had to pay attention to me, at least for few moments. This was the start of a pattern of seeking attention in the wrong ways. It would be years before I'd break that pattern.

Looking back, I can see that my arrival wasn't the "blessed event" we like to think babies' births are. My mother, Dylis, was a very young woman, working in a factory when she met a soldier named Dennis Rees. Their time together was brief, but obviously eventful, and Dennis had moved to Scotland by the time my mother discovered she was pregnant. She went to visit him in Scotland and they stayed together for a few weeks before she returned to Birmingham, and moved in with one of her sisters. She was 21 when I was born and after she had me we moved around a lot between the sisters. My mother always told me she never wanted me, that I was an accident. But on one occasion, when I was about four years old, I was something of a fortunate accident for my mother. We were at a place called Bingley Hall, an exhibition center in Birmingham. I was in a wheelchair, my legs in plaster casts with a metal bar between my feet to keep my legs apart after my most recent surgery. A lot of people noticed and expressed concern or pity, but in a kind way. As an incentive to get people to come and spend time there, the operators of Bingley Hall would hide paper stars around the exhibition center, and people who found them would win prizes. On this day, a man who'd taken notice of me kept nudging my mother, to show her where the stars were hidden. She found one and redeemed it…for 50 pounds! 50 pounds back then was equivalent to about 250 U.S. dollars, quite a lot of money in those days.

It was around that time, when I was four that we moved in with a man named Jack Sarjant. My mother must have known him for a long time because I can't ever remember him not being around. When my mother and I started living with him my mother began using Sarjant as her last name, although she and Jack didn't marry until I was fifteen years old. He adopted me then and at fifteen, I became Tony Sarjant.

We moved around a lot, to various neighborhoods and suburbs in and around Birmingham, and my mother and Jack went out a lot. As Jack's sister, whom I knew as Aunt Rose would say, "They just like to lead the good life." Of course it wasn't really a good life. My parents spent most of the money they came by on having a good time. They bought things on credit but weren't terribly keen on paying the bills. Bailiffs visiting to collect the money or the furniture, was a regular occurrence. More than once my parents would move the furniture out before the bailiffs arrived. But while the house didn't have furniture all the time, there were always parties. My parents loved giving parties and would roll back the carpets so there would be room for everyone to dance. They much preferred their busy social lives to caring for a crippled child. But I didn't mind much. Nan Sarjant looked after me.

That's what I called Jack's mother; Nan. From the first, she accepted me as her grandson, and was the first person who showed me real love. She read to me, took me places, and just let me know that I was important to her. I liked Aunt Rose too. I remember her holding a party for the Queen's Jubilee in 1952 when I was five. Nan made sure I got to attend and I remember it being a grand time. When I was in trouble with my parents and put in my room upstairs for punishment, Nan would bring food up to me and spend time with me. I spent at least half of this period of my life in hospital, but when I was home Nan took care of me and loved me.

Until I was eight. One day some very serious-looking men came to the house and put Nan on a stretcher. She looked as though she was sleeping. They carried her out to an ambulance and drove off. She died on the way to the hospital. Now I was really alone. And what was worse nothing was said to me other than, "Nan's gone." I'd never even told her good-bye. I felt empty, and I ran away.

I don't remember what I did or where I stayed; after a few days I returned home. My mother said, "Oh, you're here." That was it. I wondered what was wrong with me, that I was so unimportant to my mother and stepfather, that I was such a burden to them. Aunt Rose assured me that my problems weren't my fault. My parents "just liked to lead the good life."

* * *

Most of my schooling was in hospital. Or I should say, most of the schooling that I attended consistently was in hospital. When I was home I became a truant at a very early age. School was awful for me. I was too different from the other kids, in too many ways. I couldn't walk properly. I couldn't run at all, so playing games or sports was out of the question and watching other kids play was torture. So was the way a lot of the kids treated me. Children can be quite cruel, and my schoolmates often were. Each time I came back from a hospital stay I had plaster casts on my legs. If I didn't have casts, I was in braces; sometimes to my knees, sometimes all the way to my ankles. I always needed crutches to get around and other kids loved kicking me off my crutches; they thought it was a bit of fun. I don't know if they did it meanly or even deliberately, but it was great for a laugh when it happened; for them, not me. It taught me very early that the only person I could trust was me.

But I wasn't one to suffer in silence, exactly. As my schoolmates tormented me, I tormented my teachers. I had a very quick wit, and what we now would call a very smart mouth. I didn't know how to control either of them, and I don't think I would have controlled them if I had known. It was my way of having some control over my world. In class I spouted off whatever clever thing occurred to me. That led to a lot of formal correction, which in those days meant corporal punishment. Caning and slippering were quite common in English schools then and crutches, braces and plaster casts didn't make me immune. I was caned and slippered quite often. One evening, when I was around eight years old I was taking a bath before bedtime and my mother happened to see that I was black and blue with bruises all down my back from the slippering I'd gotten at school that day. The next day she went to school with me and went straight up to the teacher and berated him for beating me. It's the only time I can ever remember my mother standing up for me. But it didn't keep me from getting beaten again, many times.

It seems I was always the one in trouble in class and, in truth I brought it on myself. I was always commenting on what I saw as the humor in things and it really was quite disruptive in the classroom. I wasn't openly disrespectful to the teachers, in that I didn't aim my smart remarks at them, or even at the other kids. When I told jokes at someone's expense the butt of the jokes was always me. I was often the butt of the jokes other kids told as well. I knew who the joke was aimed at when two kids sitting on either side of me shared this witty exchange:

"What do you call a load of spastics in a swimming pool? Vegetable soup." They seemed to think that because my legs didn't work my head didn't work. My head worked quite well, but not in positive ways.

I was in the public schools from the time I was eight until I was eleven years old. And while I wasn't a very good student I was becoming more and more street-wise. I was learning how to survive on my own terms. And I was finding more and more ways of getting into trouble. Stealing became almost as normal as breathing, particularly stealing from shops. It didn't matter to me that if someone saw me taking something I couldn't run away with it. Stealing gave me control, I thought, and it got the other kids to look at me differently. I guess it raised my standing in their eyes. And I didn't always just take things when no one was looking. Sometimes I'd craft ways of outsmarting the system. It was common in those days, the 1950s, in England for shops to have bins of biscuits (cookies) out along the sidewalk. A favorite of kids were the "penny biscuits," the ones that were broken. Sometimes I'd tell a shopkeeper I wanted some penny biscuits and when he'd say they didn't have any penny biscuits that day, I'd put my hand in the bin, crunch up some of the "good" ones and say, "Well, now you have!" The shopkeepers were never amused when I did this but I was always quite pleased with myself.

It was things like this that kept me going; I had to use my humor to deal with life and as I've said, sometimes my humor was at my own expense. It didn't matter to me that I was laughing at myself because a lot of the time I was the only kid who was there. It wasn't that I didn't have many friends; I really didn't have any friends. I was never around long enough to make become friends with any of the other kids. I never experienced a complete fall-to-summer school year without interruption. Because of surgeries I missed three to six months of class during each of the four years I attended public schools. When I was between the ages of seven and ten I had one or two operations every year. As I was a growing child, the doctors had to keep breaking and turning the bones in my foot and leg to straighten the club foot; bone grafts and skin grafts and all that. It was a routine I knew, although I can't say I liked it. In fact, at ten I was fed up. I decided there was no way I was going to let anyone operate on me ever again. The only thing I'd known as a child was pain. I didn't know how to react to anything else.

I knew all about lying in bed crying from the pain. I knew all about kids picking on me for no reason I could see at the time. Because I was different, the kid on crutches who couldn't run away or fight back or chase after them.

But one remarkable thing did happen during that time. During one of the operations I had the sense of watching what was going on, as though I were above the doctors and nurses as they performed the surgery. Later on I described what I'd seen to Professor Allen, the surgeon who headed the operating team. I told him, in great detail, what I'd seen. He was quite astonished. He told me I had very accurately described what had gone on while I was unconscious from the anesthesia. It made me feel good, to be able to tell him what he and the others had done, to describe the tools and instruments they used. I told him, "I didn't realize you used hammers and chisels and all that." I hadn't seen these things when I was brought into the operating theater, and a child would have no concept of the equipment used in performing the surgery. I still think that experience was an amazing gift, to have some measure of control through the knowledge I'd gained from this vision, or whatever it was.

Professor Allen was the central figure in a Christmas celebration that wasn't terribly festive for me. I was in hospital about to undergo yet another surgery, and the staff served a big Christmas dinner for all the children. And Professor Allen, my surgeon, carved the turkey just two days before he was going to carve on me. I suppose I remember that small detail after all this time because he was the only person there who knew me at all. My mother wasn't there, being too busy with her own life. She was working in a factory then and when she wasn't working she and my stepfather were hosting the sorts of parties that appealed more to them. They were both drinking a lot during that time.

That was their life. I remember many times being sent upstairs to my room as the guests began arriving, the carpets being rolled back so everyone could dance. It was good times for the grownups downstairs. I could hear the music playing downstairs, the grownups enjoying themselves as I'd open the window, climb out onto the flat roof and make my way off to do what I wanted to do.

The only way I could make friends, I felt, was by doing something different from what my parents were doing. And that's what got me into stealing, and by that I mean more than just penny biscuits.

Real Trouble

It got pretty serious pretty quickly. I wasn't any more than ten years old when I acted as the lookout one night while more nimble kids broke into a shop, grabbed some stuff and ran off. Of course I couldn't run anywhere so I got caught. It never occurred to me that as the lookout, I would be the closest one to the police or whoever came to catch us, which meant I had no chance of even trying to hobble away. Even bright kids aren't very good at imagining let alone considering things like that. But I don't know that it would have mattered if I had thought of the possible consequences. When you want to please others, when you want to make friends, you'll do just about anything so the others will like you. I had decided, without knowing it that I would pay any price to be part of a group. I'd learn later just how high the price could be and how long it would take me to pay it off.

I got caught a lot but most times I was just given a warning and told not to do anything like that again, then sent on my way. Often as not I was wearing my braces to keep my foot straight from the latest operation, and I think that won me some leniency from the authorities. "Oh, the poor little crippled kid," or something like that. Of course by the time I was ten I'd learned very well how to play on adults' sympathies. I could look much more sad than guilty when I was brought into the police station. The tough cops who asked, "What's wrong with you, son," would soften even more when I'd say "I've got polio, sir." As I've said, I was getting quite street-wise.

I would never tell on anybody else. Not ever. I don't think it was a point of honor with me as much as it was not wanting to do anything that would cause me to lose my friends. This was proof of my loyalty to them, as I saw it. Even when I was brought in for things I hadn't done, I never protested and told on the others. I never actually broke into the shops; I never even went inside. But you wouldn't know that from reading my juvenile court record. It begins with "shop-breaking and stealing" early in 1958. "Office-breaking and stealing" a few months later. And there were many others that never came to court, when I was just warned.

What was ironic in all this is that, as much as I wanted to be different from my mother and stepfather I was actually tremendously influenced by them. As I've said, it was common for the bailiffs to come to our home to collect money or furniture because my parents were behind on the payments. It was also common for my parents to haul things out the back door to hide them from the bailiffs who were coming to the front door, then bring those things back into the house through the back after the bailiffs left after another unsuccessful attempt to collect a store's merchandise or money. The lesson which I was learning very well was that rules were to be ignored and those in authority were to be deceived. It was alright to do things like this; it was natural. I cannot remember any sort of moral code in my parents' home. I knew there was unspoken acceptance, even approval, if I decided to do some stealing. Of course the proceeds of that stealing were appreciated too. What sort of path does that lay out for a child? The path that I was on.

There were limits to what I would do, however. I wouldn't steal from houses. I guess because I understood that "real people" lived there. Although I would, unfortunately, be the lookout when other kids were breaking into houses. I don't know if I ever felt badly about that. In any case it was what I felt I had to do to have friends, to be part of a group. But from the earliest I never had any qualms about stealing from any sort of business, from the smallest shops to big firms. They had money. Those were the places where people like us went to take what we wanted, what we needed. It was natural.

Of course what a child does naturally, instinctively, is often what adults with mature judgment recognize as very antisocial. A child will do anything that leads to an immediate solution, with no thought for the consequences. A child will tell the most fantastic lies, never realizing how transparent those lies might be. What's remarkable, and terribly harmful, is that too often adults who should know better will go along, rather than question the child.

For example, around the time I started getting into trouble that drew the authorities' attention, I was sent on a Boys Brigade outing in Wales, about 200 miles from our home in Birmingham. The Boys Brigade was a church group and I quickly decided I didn't want to be with them in Wales, so I left. Believe it or not, I made my way all the way to London then back home again, a physically disabled ten-year old! Not that this was the first time. By the age of ten I'd learned how to cover a lot of ground on my own, hitchhiking and taking trains.

I'd started "jumping" trains when I was around seven years old. Mostly I'd ride down to London, about 120 miles from home. Getting on the trains required some inventiveness. Much of the time I'd steal some money so I could buy a ticket. If I didn't have any money I'd tell the conductor my aunt was waiting for me down in London and he'd let me on. On the train it was pretty simple to just sit at the back of the car looking sad and lonely, striking a sympathetic and generous chord with other passengers. I had blond hair, blue eyes and those crooked feet. I looked like a little crippled angel. Many times the story about my "aunt" (who didn't exist) meeting the train in London worked and no one questioned me further. Other times the police would be waiting for me at the train station in London. It never took more than a few hours for the London police to find me, although one time when I got to London I found a pastry wagon (delivery truck) headed north, so I got myself something to eat *and* a ride back to Birmingham. There was a train called the "milk train" that left London at two in the morning for the run up to Birmingham. The guard on the milk train took to bringing an extra sandwich or two with him because he knew that every couple of weeks or so I would turn up.

That was my life for a time; traveling around by myself. Sure it was lonely, but I'd come to feel that a lot of time, being by myself was the best thing for me. No one could hurt me if I was by myself. London was a wonderful world for me; a world created in my child's imagination. I really didn't do anything but walk around and look at the shops and the parks and the people. While I was there I could, in my mind, have everything I didn't have at home, except the one thing I really wanted and needed. I was looking for love, although I didn't know it at the time. No one in Birmingham really liked me. I don't mean they disliked me in a mean way. But I was terribly inconvenient to have around. Because of the disabilities I couldn't keep up the way other kids my age could, with other kids or with adults. It was better for everyone when I wasn't around. I can't remember knowing the names of more than two or three kids before I was sixteen, and that was for the wrong reasons.

"The wrong reasons" also describes the ways I got attention and what I thought was approval. I was a very precocious and bright child, although not bright in a "school" way. But I was intuitive and too clever by half. I had a quick wit and an even quicker mouth which I couldn't keep shut, not that I wanted to. As I mentioned earlier, my humorous remarks weren't mean or directed at others so the other kids always got a big laugh from the things I had to say. The teachers never did but no matter how much the price of disapproval went up, from sharp glances, to erasers being thrown at my head, to canings in front of the class, the payoff of approval from the other kids was always worth whatever price I had to pay. For that matter, so was the payoff of being noticed by the teachers. At least they knew I was there and they responded to my presence. At home I wasn't much different from the furniture, as far as my mother and stepfather were concerned. They weren't mean to me; they were indifferent. It truly did not matter to them whether I was there or not.

There was a darkly humorous and at the same time, just terribly dark side to my getting under the teachers' skin. Even when punishment extended to canings, I never showed any sign that I felt any pain; no wincing or grimacing, no crying out and, most certainly no tears. In truth, I couldn't really feel it much. The polio had left my lower body mostly numb, so the canings truly did not hurt very much at all. I remember one time I received "six of the best" in front of the whole school on a Friday afternoon. When the teacher was done caning me I said, "Thank you very much," and he bent me over for six more! He really put everything into those six and I know he was trying to make me cry, to show me and the other students what happened to kids who smarted off. I didn't make a sound, or get red in the face or shed any tears.

What that teacher didn't know is that he could have caned me until his arm went limp and I wouldn't have cried. I hadn't cried since I was a very young child in hospital. I decided, subconsciously that crying was something I couldn't afford to do. I knew somehow that if I was going to survive, it would be the only way I knew how to do it. I couldn't give up control over my emotions, my feelings. I couldn't let anyone else know that I was sad or unhappy. Of course, refusing to cry means refusing to give up any of that sadness and unhappiness; it turns life into a struggle, every day of your life. In time you start asking yourself, quite seriously, if you can continue that struggle or if you even want to. It's why, as a child of ten, I started having thoughts of suicide. Who was I and why did I have to be so different from everyone else? Why couldn't I run and do the things all the other kids did? Why was I such a failure? Had I just been bad from the beginning? Is that why I got polio, why I had crooked feet and all the rest?

All the rest. The other kids had the same names as their parents. Not me. My mother's name (at the least the name she used) was Sarjant; my name was Rees. And kids notice *everything*. They'd ask, "Why don't you have the same name as your Mum? Is she your *real* Mum?" I didn't know how to answer. All I knew was that it wasn't fair. I started thinking nothing was fair. All I could see was hate. And I soon started hating who and what I was. I must have done something to deserve all this. Being kicked off my crutches; being laughed at, called "cripple" and "spastic." And not having anyone to go to and talk about it, no one who cared, or even listened. What was the best way out? Death. But I decided I didn't want to die. I wanted a life on *my* terms. I decided to get smart. I decided I would get recognition, one way or another, even if it meant doing things I shouldn't do. And that's what I did…a lot.

Being the "poor little crippled kid" had always given me a sort of immunity from getting into really serious legal trouble. But as I got older and the police took me in more and more, that immunity started wearing off. I don't know whether anyone was using the phrase "known to authorities" in the mid to late 1950s, but the authorities definitely knew who I was. I was the kid who was often outside the shop or factory when a bunch of kids broke in and stole stuff from it. I was getting picked up and brought in for questioning more and more. Much of the time the police brought me in for things I wasn't involved with. But a lot of the time they hauled me in for questions about robberies that happened when I *was* there. I'd become a Usual Suspect.

I'd developed a rather twisted attitude of honesty. If police asked me a direct question, I would tell the truth. But they had to ask *very* direct questions; questions such as, "Were you standing lookout when that shop down the block was robbed the other night?" If I'd been watching for people while the other kids were robbing the place I'd say, "Yes." But if the questions weren't that direct I'd play verbal cat-and-mouse with the cops all day and feel quite proud of myself for doing it.

One day as I was coming out of school the police picked me up and took me to the station. They said they'd seen me break into the school. I blamed other people, without naming names. I told the police I'd seen other kids running away from the school at night. "Are you sure," one of the cops said, "are you sure it was other kids and not you who broke in?" My conscience wouldn't let me keep up the lie. "Yes," I said, "it was me."

It was one of the few times I'd done the actual breaking-and-entering, and I'd been by myself. I think I wanted revenge on a place I hated. I knew there was no money in the school, nothing to take. I just wanted to be there on my own terms. I didn't steal anything or vandalize the place. I broke in, stayed awhile, then left. That's what I told the police, and they knew I was telling the truth. No real damage was done, and they sent me home with a warning to stay out of trouble.

I didn't listen. Two nights later some kids broke into a shop while I stood lookout. The police were waiting for me when I got out of school the next day. They knew I'd been involved and they wanted to know who else was there, who was inside the shop doing the stealing. I wouldn't tell them. Again, I said I saw some kids running away but I couldn't see who they were. This was my way of protecting people I thought were my friends. It was also my way of protecting myself. Some of these kids were pretty hard cases and I have no doubt I would have paid a very high price if I'd named names to the police. Of course the police knew I was lying. They tried to induce me to tell them who'd done the actual stealing, promising me little or no punishment if I'd identify the other kids. As it turned out, I paid a very high price for keeping quiet. Eventually, instead of just getting a "slap on the wrist," I was sent to an Approved School. I didn't care. People were noticing me. I mattered.

(One of the kids involved that night grew up to become very accomplished in his profession. Years later he contacted me and said he appreciated my silence about that night. He also said he'd stopped stealing after learning that I'd been caught. I don't know whether my misfortune had anything to do with his turning away from juvenile crime.)

A Season in Hell

Number 101.

That was me. At the age of eleven I became Number One-Oh-One at an approved school in Birmingham, one of more than a hundred kids there. Before very long I came to think of 101 as my name; that or Rees, never Tony.

The court authorities said they were sending me to "a place of safety." They said I'd be safer there than I had been at home or on the street. I wasn't.

I'd been at the approved school about six weeks when, one night a couple of the bigger kids came and woke me. "Come with us," they said. They walked on either side of me and led me into the bathroom, where one of the school guards was standing. Then without anyone saying anything, the two boys pushed me down onto the floor and held me there while the guard sexually assaulted me. When he was finished he changed places with one of the boys, who took his turn, then the other did.

I was sick, shocked, numb, disgusted, terrified. And what I heard next was as bad as what had just happened.

Someone, I don't know who, said, "Don't you say nothin' about this, or we'll kill you. No one'll care. No one likes you anyway. No one'll miss you."

They were right. I knew I couldn't call out, didn't dare go to anyone about what happened. I just had to survive and I had to do it myself, had to do whatever it took to stay alive. Somewhere inside me I had this fighting instinct that said to the world, "Whatever you do to me, I'm gonna get back up and I'm gonna keep getting back up no matter what." That state of mind is probably what kept me from thinking about the reality. I was eleven years old, small and physically weak. I walked with a very pronounced limp. I couldn't fight back much against kids my own size, and these kids were bigger and stronger. They were almost the size of grown-ups. The guard was an adult. Any one of them could have overpowered me by himself. I was completely helpless against three of them. Every night.

Days in the approved schools of that time (what in America were then called reform schools) were a dull routine of classes from eight in the morning until three in the afternoon, then back to our dormitories until mealtimes. We were always inside, never outdoors. There was a point system that rewarded good behavior; privileges granted when you got to 100 points. I don't know what the rewards were. I never came anywhere near to 100 points, because my behavior during the day was never good. I couldn't fight back against what was happening to me at night so I fought back during the day, in every way I could. In an institution full of confused and angry young boys, I was very angry and confused indeed.

Whenever I could I'd sneak off for a smoke (I'd started smoking when I was nine), and to think. Why was this happening to me every night? Was it normal? Was *I* normal? I didn't know. I didn't know what to feel. Before long I didn't feel anything, not even pain. A year earlier I thought I wanted to be dead. Now I felt dead, I guess. Or like a block of wood. Block. That's what I did. I blocked out what was happening. Always the same guard, always the same kids.

Looking back, those kids must have started out as his victims. After I got a little bigger the guard started asking me to "help" him with younger kids. He kept after me to help him until the day I was released from the approved school after three years of custody. I never did; there was no way I ever would.

People who study them say rapists aren't after sex; they're after power. I certainly believe that was what this guard wanted. The emotional torment he inflicted was at least as bad as the physical torment. He'd say, "You know you can't tell anyone, don't you? Who'd believe you, right? A little crippled thief; no one's gonna believe anything you tell 'em."

I believed every word of what he said. I couldn't trust anyone to help me. He was someone who was supposed to keep me "safe," someone I was supposed to trust. But I couldn't trust him. I couldn't trust anyone. Before long I couldn't even believe anyone, couldn't believe the world held anything but harm for me.

One day the approved school had a royal visitor, Princess Margaret, the younger sister of Queen Elizabeth. We'd all cleaned up and looked our best to meet Her Highness. We stood at attention in a long line as she walked past. She barely nodded at most of the boys, but when she saw me said, "My, what a nice-looking boy," or something like that. I should have felt like the proudest boy in England, but I felt nothing. How could she mean it? How could there be anything good about someone who did what I did every night. It never occurred to me that I wasn't doing anything; it was being done *to* me.

The nights were the worst, of course. But the approach of nighttime was awful as well. I'd begin to get anxious as late afternoon gave way to evening, knowing what was to come after the sun went down and all the boys had gone to bed. And even after the assaults were over, they were never completely over. Back in my bed I'd have trouble falling asleep, and once asleep the nightmares would come and the attacks would repeat, over and over. This went on for years, even well into adulthood. The nightmares wouldn't stop until I was past 40.

Pre-adolescence is a confusing time for everyone, but much more so for me. I had no clues about my sexual identity. I was in a school prison with more than a hundred other boys. I'd never had any male role models, no one to look to for guidance as to what a man should be like. I certainly hadn't had any sexual experiences before entering the approved school. I'd heard the words "queer" and "faggot" and I'd formed a rather dim impression that these words applied to men who acted like women somehow. Is that what I was? I didn't know. I understood that to be this way was not a good thing and in spite of my delight in seeing myself as an outlaw, I never really wanted to be a bad person. I wanted to be good. Was that not possible now? I didn't know.

I must have been taught some vocational skills during the more than three years I was in the approved school, certainly some classroom skills, but I don't remember any of them. Unconsciously but deliberately, I made that time of my life a blur in my mind. I remember the assaults, but not the details. And I remember next to nothing, not even general, vague memories of other things that happened there. I was barely more than a little boy when I was sent in and was on the brink of starting to become a young man when I was let out, but it happened without me noticing at all. I can never remember Christmases there, although we must of have had them. I can never remember birthdays, but we must have had them. All I can remember is one, long night. When I came out of the approved school at fifteen, I truly had no idea who or what I was.

A New Life?

I was released to the supervision of my stepfather, Jack Sarjant, who really was my stepfather by then. He and my mother had recently gotten married so she legally had his name and so did I, since he had adopted me. I didn't feel like I was part of a family because, except in the strictly legal sense, I wasn't. Jack Sarjant adopting me was just a formality, to go along with marrying my mother, more than ten years after they'd started living together.

They were working at a golf course then, managing the golf club. I worked there too sometimes. Just long enough to make a little money; and long enough to steal money from my mother. That's what I did most. I stole in part for revenge against my mother. She'd told me early on that she never wanted me, and her behavior toward me always bore that out. So if she wouldn't give me love I'd see to it that she provided me with money, whether she knew it or not. And besides, I needed money. I'd met a girl.

Her name was Carol and she was about a year older than me. Her family lived far enough from the golf course that I needed to drive there. I didn't have a car, so I'd take one of the taxis assigned to the golf course and pay the fare with the money I stole from my mother. I always took the same taxi and I told Carol that it was one of my family's cars and the driver was my personal driver. She believed me, and why not? I'd also told her my parents owned the golf course.

Carol was the first person I'd had a relationship with since Nan Sarjant died when I was eight. It wasn't a sexual relationship; in fact I don't even know that our relationship was romantic. Carol was my friend, the first real friend I ever had. We just talked mostly. What was truly amazing to me is that she listened! She actually wanted to know what I had to say. I can't remember what I told her; lies no doubt. But our time together was wonderful. Someone was genuinely interested in me. Of course it couldn't last; I made sure of that. My mother discovered that money was missing from the restaurant. When she asked me if I knew anything about it I told her, "Yes, I took it". She promptly had me arrested and I was ordered to spend two more years in an approved school. Before being sent off I told Carol I was going to train for the Merchant Navy. She was very excited for me.

I actually didn't lie to her completely. The approved school I was sent to was a place that aimed to teach boys how to really be men and to learn how to contribute to society in a good way. We *were* being trained to serve in the Merchant Navy. We wore uniforms and were learning skills vital to being merchant seamen. For the first time in my life I was doing something positive, something with a real future that I could see for myself. The authorities felt that I was physically fit enough for this particular school and I loved it. I really took to the training and for the first time ever, I was keeping up with everyone else. Naturally, it didn't last. It was decided that I was not physically fit enough to actually serve in the Merchant Navy. I would keep training while I finished my sentence at the approved school, but I wouldn't be assigned to a ship afterward. I didn't see any point in continuing to train, so the first chance I got I took off. I went to visit Carol. I wore my uniform and told her I was in the Merchant Navy. She told me I looked grand and I could see she was really happy for me. I told her I'd come to see her when I was home from sea duty. She said she'd look forward to hearing all about life on board ship. Not long after that I became horribly sick. I had an attack of appendicitis and my appendix burst. I'd never felt so awful. I thought I was going to die and I didn't want the last thing I told Carol to be a pack of lies. I somehow got to her house and I told her the truth about me; everything. That my parents didn't own a golf course; that I wasn't going off to serve in the Merchant Navy; that other than my name, nothing I'd told her was the truth. Then I waited for her to tell me to get out. But she didn't. She told me she was glad I'd decided to tell her the truth and that we were still friends. She said we'd still be friends after I cleared up my legal troubles. I couldn't believe what I was hearing. Carol was standing by me. No one had ever done that. I don't know if I prayed, but I knew I didn't want to die; I wanted to get well. I had something to live for. And I began to recover. Soon I was well; well enough to sabotage the good thing that was happening in my life. Another kid and I stole a car and were quickly caught and packed off. Carol heard about it and, sadly and correctly decided we weren't really friends.

What I'd done with Carol is something I did over and over with "good people" who came into my life. Subconsciously but deliberately I did things to kill the relationships. I was pushing them away from me, for their protection and mine. If people were close to me then I had to worry about them; I had some responsibility for them. And I knew I wasn't a responsible person at all, so it was best for them (I told myself) if they weren't around me. And it was best for me because it meant there was one less thing for me to fail at.

There was another reason I had to end it with Carol or, more to the point, make sure she ended it. We had actually gotten engaged to be married, but we'd never been sexually intimate. It wasn't that I was shy about sex; I was terrified. Because of what had happened to me in the approved school, the years of being forcibly raped every night, I regarded sex as violence. The very act of sex was a matter of one person attacking another. I couldn't stand the thought of me attacking Carol, and it never occurred to me then to see sex any other way, so things had to end between us.

* * *

One night when I was running from the police, I ran into the arms of a higher authority. I don't remember what I'd done but the cops were chasing me through a park. I saw a crowd going into a big tent and I figured I'd have a better chance of not getting arrested if I could hide amongst all the people, so I got into the crowd and let myself get swept along into the tent, not knowing what sort of a show was going on inside. It turned out to be very different from anything I had ever seen or could have imagined.

It was a Billy Graham crusade. The famous American evangelist was preaching in Bristol that week. I'd never seen or felt anything like the atmosphere inside that enormous tent. I'd certainly never heard anything like the Reverend Graham's preaching and when he invited people to come forward and give their lives to Christ, I found myself leaving the seats and walking toward the pulpit, along with dozens of other people. At the time I told myself I was just making sure I stayed in the crowd (and after "accepting" Christ in front of the pulpit, I left the tent and was on the run again). But years later I began to wonder if there wasn't some part of me that really was touched by the Reverend Graham's invitation to come to Christ that night. I didn't know it that night, but I believe he planted a seed, one that took many years to germinate.

I managed to give the cops the slip that night. But a few weeks later my luck ran out. I'd fallen in with another boy about my age and I stood watch while he broke into a house. That night ended with both of us in custody. The court decided we were too hard for any approved school so we were both ordered to a detention center, which is exactly what it sounds like; jail. Three months in jail. It was long enough for me to learn that I didn't care to spend any more time in places like that. After I was released I looked for a real job.

* * *

The British economy was very strong in the mid-1960s. You could pretty much walk off one job and into another in the same day, and sometimes that's just what I did. I had about ten different jobs between the ages of sixteen and 21. I worked in a shoe shop, a toy shop, in one of the biggest department stores in England. If I didn't work in a place where there were a lot of employees, I'd work in a business where a lot of customers came everyday. I needed to have people around me, and that's how I made sure it happened. I really liked some of the jobs I had; others I hated. But even in jobs I liked my employment always ended badly. I loved working as a chef and got good training for this in several restaurants, but I'd always self-destruct. I'd subconsciously arrange circumstances so that staying would become intolerable, either for me or for my employer or both. I didn't feel that I was worthy of having anything good in my life, so I had to see to it that the good things didn't last. And if I couldn't sabotage my situation at work, I'd do something stupid away from work.

The lesson I'd learned during three months in the detention center evidently wore off. A few months after I turned 20 I stole a car; I was caught and given a sentence of probation, no jail if I didn't get into any more trouble. Of course I did. Less than six months later I was caught breaking into the golf club where my parents worked. That resulted in me being sentenced to the Borstal Training Center until I was no longer a juvenile. Luckily for me I guess, that was only four months away. I was released on my 21st birthday. The staff at Borstal were glad to see me go. The nightmares were very bad while I was there. The guards could see something was really bothering me, but I wouldn't tell them what. The counselors asked me about it, but I wouldn't tell them either. What was the point? No one would believe me. But all those feelings came back, every afternoon as the sunlight started to fade. During the night I slept little, and poorly. When the room would begin to get lighter as the sun started coming up, I'd feel like something that had been pushing me down all night started to lift. "Finding joy in the new day" was more than just a nice phrase for me. The attacks had ended years before, but the fear would go on for decades.

As you might expect, my mother and stepfather weren't very keen on having me live with them, even if I'd wanted to and I most certainly didn't. I struck out on my own.

I'd been referred to apply for a job at a hospital in Birmingham and I really didn't want to work there. I was trying to think of the sort of lie I could tell that would make them not want to hire me, when I got an inspiration. I'll tell them the truth!

So there I was, interviewing with the Hospital Administrator and for the first time in my life I was telling the truth about myself. I told him where I'd just been, in custody at Borstal. I told him about my criminal history, the times and places I'd been confined. It all just came out of me in a rush and I felt wonderful. It was such a relief not to lie. It was a relief knowing I wouldn't have to remember what lies I'd told. And it was a relief knowing that there was no way I'd get a job working there. But I wasn't prepared for what the administrator said. He told me, "I'm impressed by your honesty. Most boys in your position would lie about their past. I'd like you to work for me." I was shocked, to say the least. I reluctantly accepted his offer.

I was working as a porter, or orderly in what's called the surgical theater in British hospitals, the operating room in the U.S. As it turned out, this was one of the first good things that happened to me. I found the hospital to be a place where I could act the way I really felt, because that's what others around me were doing. It was a place where I could feel down when things were sad and laugh when things were funny. And I met someone who, almost instantly, became a real friend.

Her name was Christine. We were chatting at work one day and she asked me if I knew of anyone who needed a place to live because she needed a roommate, someone to share expenses. I told her I needed a place and she said, "Well, come on then. You can bring your things over and move in tonight." So I did, but I was quite wary. I didn't want to get into another relationship and end up hurting someone the way I'd done with Carol. As it turned out, I had no reason to worry.

Christine was a lesbian, the first I ever met. I didn't really even know what the word meant when she first told me. Public attitudes at that time weren't as "open" and tolerant as what we've all come to expect, and Christine felt the need to be discreet about her sexual preference. It was never an issue for me, nor was it something we discussed or needed to. She was my roommate and my friend, the first real friend I ever had. We went just about everywhere together; to movies, to dinner, to the park. The people at work, people we'd meet socially or casually all assumed we were a couple, seeing how much we enjoyed one another's company. What they were seeing were two people who could be completely natural with one another. I didn't have to worry about sexual activity, committing what I thought was violence against a woman I liked. She didn't have to worry about men coming on to her, and making excuses that could lead to her having to "confess" her homosexuality. Ours was the safest of relationships for both of us.

Safe or not, after about nine months I felt very strongly that I needed to get away. This was the pattern of much of my early adult life. I had to be on the run.

I didn't know I could never get away from what I was running from; I was running from myself.

I took a job with Butlin's at Clacton-on-Sea. Butlin's is the best-known resort company in England, and the resort at Clacton-on Sea, on the English Channel east of London, was hugely popular then. I couldn't have known it at the time, but going to work in the vacation/holiday industry would in some small way lay the very early groundwork of what would save my life many years later. Unlike my interview at the hospital, I really wanted this job so I did what I'd always done to get what I wanted. I lied. I made up stuff about my experience, my personal and professional history; it was quite impressive. I got a job as an assistant manager, running one of the restaurants inside the resort.

I worked at Butlin's through the summer season and when the season ended I went back to Birmingham. I stayed out of trouble with the law, but legal trouble was just one of a lot of things that were missing from my life. More than anything, I guess I must have felt I had to have control over things. And that's what led me back to the occult.

The Dark Side

I'd had my first experience with the occult when I was ten years old. I'd gone with my mother to see a woman who read tea leaves. I was fascinated, watching this old woman peering down at soggy tea leaves lying on a plate. And then she looked up at me and she told my mother I'd soon be going away for a long time. Not too many months later I was sent off to the approved school.

I played around with ouija boards when I was a teenager. I'd get some kids together and conduct séances. I felt a real sense of power, seeing how the other kids would look at me while I "summoned and controlled spirits." I thought it was great fun and I loved the feeling of control. But one time something happened that really scared me. I was leading a séance and I told another kid's girlfriend that, in three days her grandmother would die; I even told her the time of day it would happen. I didn't know why I said it or where I got the idea for the time; I was just playing, but I loved seeing the look on the girl's face. I'd forgotten all about it, until I saw the girl's boyfriend a few days later. He looked at me very strange, like he was afraid of me. That was odd. No one was afraid of me.

"What's wrong with you?" I asked.

"My girl's gran died," he said, very quietly.

"Go on! She didn't!"

"She did. Right when you said she would."

We just looked at each other, neither of us saying anything for what seemed like a very long time.

"I gotta go," he said finally, "I'll see you 'round."

"Yeah," I said absently, "See ya."

He and I didn't see each other much at all after that.

I was really scared for about a week or so. For the first few days afterward I told myself I was through with ouija boards and séances and the like. But the fear quickly faded and that feeling of power came back to me. Power! That's something I never had, and although I didn't think about it consciously I knew I couldn't give it up. I became obsessed with the occult; horoscopes, fortune-telling, palm-reading, tarot cards, crystal balls. It was all incredibly seductive.

Years later, not long after I returned to Birmingham from Butlin's, I was in a pub one night and I ran across a guy I'd gone to school with. We talked about what we'd done since we were kids. He probably told me a bunch of lies. I know that's what I told him, mostly. He asked what I was doing and at that point I told the truth. "I'm not doin' nothin.'" I told him how I'd just gotten back into town, what I'd been doing at Butlin's. I don't know how the subject came up, but he must have sensed that what I wanted more than a job, was power; power over other people. He invited me to join what he called a secret group of "brothers."

They were Satanists and I joined up with them that night. We held regular meetings several times a week, with Satanic rituals. We drew circles, lit black candles, called up spirits and manifestations. And it worked! We could actually see what we'd summoned. And we'd get down on our knees and worship. It was intoxicating. We wanted power; power over our own lives and power to use against anyone who got in our way, the power to curse people. Little did I know how much that power would curse *me*, or for how long.

I didn't know it at the time, but my embrace of the occult aggravated something that was going on inside me and had been for years. There was the part of me that desperately wanted to succeed, to be wanted, to be loved. And then there was the part that believed I didn't deserve anything good, that I didn't even deserve to be alive. What some call the dark arts made both sides much worse.

I'd gotten a job working in a restaurant in London. It wasn't a terribly important job; cooking, cleaning, filling in wherever I was needed. But very shortly I was doing everything better than the people who'd been working at these jobs for years. And the restaurant owner noticed. One day he told me he needed someone to manage the place and he wanted me to be his manager. Would I do it; would I help him? I could hardly believe what I was hearing! Of course I would!

It seemed I knew what to do at every turn, instinctively. I'd had little training in restaurant work. I spent just about all my time in the golf course restaurant my parents managed trying to get out of work, or waiting for opportunities to steal. But now I knew how to do everything. Whenever a problem came up I had a solution in almost no time. It was like I could see things before they happened; I took full advantage of opportunities to expand business before those opportunities were apparent to anyone else. The owner said he'd never seen anyone with a better "feel" for the restaurant business; that I was a natural. He didn't know how *un*natural the source of my "talent" was.

The power and control I always wanted were coming my way. I practiced the rituals faithfully, and my "faith" was being rewarded beyond anything I had ever imagined. Before long I was running three tremendously successful restaurants in London, one of the world's great cities. Even though I knew nothing about the restaurant business! But at night, when I went home, I felt like a fraud, or worse. I didn't deserve this success, and the feelings of fear about the rituals were returning; so were the nightmares, worse than ever. But somehow, I'd survive the night and the next day I'd go back out into the world, armed with power.

I went out armed with something else; whiskey. I'd started drinking, a lot. The atmosphere of the restaurant industry seemed to invite drinking, so that's how I got started. I started drinking heavily because it was a good way to wash out the war that was going on in my mind. One part of me wanted the success I was having. Another part knew I didn't deserve it and tried to destroy it. One part of me was grateful that my life was turning out to be good. Another part knew that wasn't how my life was supposed to be. One part of me said, "Yes, you *can* do this," and another part said, "No, you can't." One part of me wanted to survive. Another part wanted to die. The whiskey was strong enough to wash away the war for a few hours, but it wasn't strong enough to drown it; so every morning before I left for work, I'd down a bottle of whiskey; and every night, before I went to bed, I'd down another. I can't remember how much I'd put away during the day; enough to land me in the hospital.

I don't recall what the doctors called it (How could I? I was drunk), but it was probably something very much like acute alcohol poisoning. They asked me how much I was drinking and I told them, as best I could. It took about a week to get my system clean from the effects of the liquor and the doctor's orders couldn't have been any clearer: No more whiskey. A few months later I collapsed at work. The people I supervised at one of the restaurants called for an ambulance and soon I was back in the hospital, near death again.

The doctor who'd overseen my care the first time was quite stern when I sobered up enough that he could talk to me with some confidence that I'd understand what he was saying.

"I thought I told you to quit drinking whiskey," he said.

"I did," I said, "I haven't had a drop in months."

"Then why are you back here?"

"Bacardi!" I smiled up at him from my hospital bed. He didn't smile back.

That's how I thought I could handle bad situations; make a joke, with me as the punch line. I actually thought the doctor would be amused that I was now making myself sick with rum instead of whiskey. He tolerated me draining off National Health resources for the few days it took to get me more or less well again, then he had me discharged. So at the age of 22 I had addicted myself to alcohol *and* the occult. It's probably not surprising that before long I was completely immersed in the occult.

Years later I attended a presentation by a "medium." This woman was the most famous "spiritualist" in England at that time, maybe in the world. She certainly didn't look the part of someone who got messages from the dead and saw into the future. She was middle-aged and looked like someone's grandmother. That was a big part of her appeal. Even her critics described her as "down to Earth." But she claimed she had a gift that was decidedly un-Earthly. I wanted to meet her. I wanted to be part of her work. And she welcomed me.

My "gifts" for organization and business expansion that served me so well in the restaurant industry were now being brought to bear on her behalf. The people around her were totally devoted to spreading her work, and I was as devoted as anyone. Soon she was performing "readings" and other acts of clairvoyance for crowds of thousands. She filled concert halls all over London and across the United Kingdom. People came to hear her tell them what jobs they should take, where they should live, whom they should marry. And they believed her. *I* believed her.

The temptation is to say it was all rubbish, but it was dangerous rubbish. This woman and others like her (and those who follow them) are treading on very unstable ground. I certainly was and in time it began to bother me so much that I recognized I was involved in something that just wasn't right. I won't go into detail, but I saw things that no one should see; things that came from a source that wasn't just unholy, but completely destructive. I saw the darkness, the desperation, the fear. The fear, I learned, is what controls the lives of people who are involved with the occult. It wasn't until years after I'd stopped having anything to do with it, until after I'd totally embraced God, that I realized just how destructive it all was.

It's ironic that what got me away from all that Evil, is the same thing that kept me from embracing Good. I simply could not (or would not) give myself to it 100-percent. Ultimately, both God and the Devil demand the same thing…total submission. For much of my life, and certainly at that time, I saw submission as surrender. And I wouldn't surrender at all. I would not give myself to anyone or anything, and while that left me totally alone and kept away people who truly wanted to help me, it helped save me.

A Family of My Own

The doctor who had disgustedly treated me for alcohol poisoning probably figured the next time me saw me I'd be lying on a slab, dead. He clearly had no patience for a very young man who seemed determined to drink himself to death, and the sooner the better. But in fact the second episode truly scared me, and I knew I had to change my life. I knew I had to get out of the environment I was in. I knew that the restaurant business would quite literally be the death of me. I went on the run again, but this time in a very different way.

About six months earlier I met a young woman named Pat. Actually I met her sister first. She worked as a waitress at one of the restaurants I was running and, in my not-at-all-humble opinion she was doing a very bad job of it so I sacked her, told her she was fired. She took it better than her sister did. Pat was a waitress at another of the restaurants I ran and the next time I was in there she confronted me.

"Why'd you sack my sister?"

She asked it in a very challenging tone, and this was a time in my life when I wouldn't be challenged by anyone. In truth, I wouldn't really listen to anyone I didn't have to listen to and in my mind that applied to anyone and everyone who wasn't a manager. Pat was just a waitress. Who was she to challenge me?

"I sacked your sister because she's a very bad worker. Now, don't *you* have work to do?" Oh, I was a delight to be around. Pat went back to her duties.

She never said anything else about her sister's sacking. Maybe she too thought that her sister wasn't a very good waitress. Anyway, our jobs forced us to work together and in time our conversations evolved from talk about work to just talk, then to talk about ourselves. We started dating. I liked her, a lot. And she liked me. Soon we were together whenever we weren't working, and often even when we were. I felt different with her than I'd ever felt before in my life. I felt like I was really "someone" in her eyes. I wasn't some young petty criminal, like I'd been when I met Carol. When Pat met me I was someone who managed restaurants. I was someone she kind of looked up to, and not just because I was a boss. Being with her I felt like a grown-up, for the first time in my life.

Pat was the first person I went to see after I got out of the hospital the second time. "I've got to leave the restaurants," I told her, "If I don't I'm gonna drink myself to death."

"What are you going to do?" she asked.

"I'm gonna get married," I said, "if you'll say 'yes.'"

I told her I felt that this was the "right" thing to do. I'd never had that feeling before in my life. She said yes. Then she said something I thought was absolutely wonderful.

"Tony, we should go to Birmingham. It's where you belong. It's where we belong."

We put our arms around each other and hugged for a very long time. A few days later we were on the train to Birmingham.

Once we got there I very quickly found a job in a hotel. Pat set about looking for a place for us to live while I went to the city offices to fill out the forms and paperwork for us to get married. A few days later Pat and I got married in the Birmingham registry office. Nobody turned up at the wedding. My mother and stepfather didn't come. Pat's parents lived in London and at the time I thought that's why they weren't there. A few years later I learned the real reason.

I was starting a new life, a life and a family all my own. For the first time I had a healthy, intimate relationship with a woman. I learned that sex was not an act of violence. I learned that being physically intimate wasn't an attack on the person I cared for more than anyone. Pat soon told me the best news I'd ever heard. We were going to have a baby. I almost couldn't believe it. A child! We really were going to be a family. And when our little girl we named Julie was born I felt so wonderful I thought I'd burst. I'd finally found happiness with this perfect, beautiful little person in my new life. But my old life, lives really, wouldn't allow it.

Soon the nightmares came back, worse than ever. Again I found myself dreading the night. I didn't want to sleep; I was sleeping only a few hours each night, getting next to no rest. Pat asked what the matter was, but I couldn't tell her. I suppose she thought I was feeling the pressure of being a new father, having to be responsible for someone besides myself. But that wasn't it. Soon I was a wreck, physically and mentally. On more than one occasion I was admitted to the hospital after collapsing emotionally. Two years after Julie was born we had a little boy. John was wonderful. If only I could have enjoyed the beautiful gift he was, he and Julie. But each day I grew more and more unwell. I could barely work; then I couldn't bear to leave the house; finally I didn't even want to get out of bed. Only a few months after the birth of our baby John, I was admitted to the Rubery Hill Asylum, a mental hospital. I'd gone crazy.

Sick as I was, I don't believe I was nearly as crazy as the doctor who was assigned to help me get well. I can't imagine what all the latest fads were in mental health treatment at that time in England, but I was totally unimpressed with what this man was doing. He apparently loved to play "let's pretend."

During one session he said, "Imagine you see a submarine coming down the road straight at you. What would you do?"

"I'd sink it with my battleship," I replied.

"Ah," he said enthusiastically, "And where did you get your battleship?"

"The same place you got your submarine," I answered.

Another time he handed me a billiard ball and said, "I want you to pretend this is an orange, and eat it." I handed it back and said, "I'll tell you what; you peel it, and I'll eat it."

Then there were the ink blot tests. "Look it this and tell me what you see," he'd say. One day I'd tell him everything was a butterfly, another day everything would be something else, but on no day did I ever tell him what anything really looked like to me. I could see a lot of things in those ink blots, but I wasn't about to tell anyone, least of all this doctor, what I saw.

I'd spent enough time around mental health treatments, during my incarcerations as a kid, to have gotten a feel for the way the game was played. I'd very quickly figure out what the psychologist or psychiatrist wanted to hear and that's what I'd say. I had no idea what this doctor wanted to hear, and to this day I'm not sure he did either. He was getting paid, but all his stupid questions and games were wasting my time. One day he told me, "Anthony," (no one called me Anthony) "I'm going to take all the pieces of your life apart, and put them back together the way they're supposed to be, so you'll be well again." That was absolutely the wrong thing to say to me. I promptly made arrangements to get myself discharged from the Rubery Hill Mental Asylum. It was an easy matter. I'd been admitted after taking a handful of tablets in a suicide attempt. I'd never tried to harm anyone else. So, since I was no danger to anyone else and I no longer displayed any suicidal tendencies, I was allowed to go home with Pat and the babies.

Not long after that, when I returned home from work one night the police were waiting for me. "Come with us," they said. I'd heard that command so many times in my life that I just reacted without thinking; I went with them. As I was being put into a cell at the police station I didn't think, "I shouldn't be here. I haven't done anything wrong." I knew that in my life I'd done enough things wrong that I could be arrested every week until I was 50 before the cops got caught up on all my earlier lawbreaking that had gone unpunished. I figured they'd found out about something I'd done and were going to question me about it until I confessed. I of course had no intention of telling them anything, but what they told me left me truly speechless.

After about ten minutes a policeman came down to my cell, opened the door and said, "Come on. We've got your so-called wife upstairs." The exact words didn't really register with me at first, and I just followed him up the stairs. I don't know why, but I thought that perhaps Pat had been caught shoplifting or something like that. Then the cop said, "Well I've got some good news or bad news, whichever way you want it. Your wife is already married." And that's how

I learned that my marriage to Pat was bigamous. A few hours later I was back in the mental hospital, after again trying to kill myself.

Why live? I no longer cared about anything. If the woman who I thought wanted to be my wife, who bore my two children, the first person I ever completely trusted and gave myself to, had lied to me and had been lying all along, what reason did I have to live? I'd lost everything. I just wanted to go to sleep forever.

I spent four weeks in the mental hospital, and during that time I realized that I had two children and I didn't want them to go through what I had in my life. So I determined that Pat and I would move and try to make this family work, to create a real home for Julie and John. I told Pat, "We're going to move." I knew we had to go somewhere else, someplace "fresh" for all of us. We moved to a small town called Daventry, a little more than 40 miles from Birmingham. It turned out to be the place where I got well, but not right away; not right away at all.

Things started to get slightly better. We found a small house to rent, and I got a job working for the ambulance service, a job I just loved. For the first time in my life I was working at helping people in a really good way. Life felt better, during the day. At night there was still the darkness inside me, the horrible dreams. It was like living in two worlds. Then my daytime world fell apart again. I found out that Pat was having an affair.

I left the ambulance service and took a job as a coach (bus) driver, driving all over Europe. This way, I told myself, Pat could have her freedom. We were still living together although I was gone for two to three weeks at a stretch. At least my kids had a home and didn't have to wonder who their father was. There was nothing between Pat and me. In truth the marriage died the day I learned she was a bigamist but I stayed married to her so I could look after my kids. They were my joy, my reason for living, and that made living this way worthwhile. Then when John was about nine years old, I found out Pat was having another affair.

That was it for me. I told Pat she could have everything, the house and whatever else she wanted or felt she needed. I suppose I could have gone to court and tried to have her declared an unfit mother or something like that, but it wouldn't have been the truth. Pat was a very good mother to our kids. She took really wonderful care of Julie and John. They were growing up to be delightful young people. So Pat and I agreed that they would live with her and I could see them whenever I wanted. Then I went on the road. I had *my* freedom, or something that felt like it.

Being a coach driver was perfect for me. It was a way out. People could see me as the jolly person at the front of the bus, laughing, telling jokes, making sure everyone was having as wonderful a time as I obviously was. It was a mask, of course. I was miserable. I just knew my life was going to screw up again. Knew it! There was no way out for me. Who wanted me? What was I worth? Nothing. Hadn't my whole life proved that? A sickly kid no one wanted, who no one loved, who grew up to be a man no one loved. I felt like what I was sure I was, a total failure. I was past 30, and alone. Still looking for the dream everyone's looking for, the happy ending. Only each day I felt more strongly that I'd never find it. No happy ending for me. So I planned for what made the most sense; an ending without the happiness. I planned everything perfectly. I just knew there was no way anyone would find me until I'd done it. I got my bottle of tablets and my drink, and drove out to a place in the country that I'd chosen because it was completely out of the way. I sat in my car and swallowed all the tablets and drank off everything in the bottle. Bye-bye, world. I don't think I'll miss you and I know you won't miss me. Four days later I came around, in the hospital. At first I thought I'd gone to Heaven, seeing soft lights all around. Then reality hit me. What would I be doing in Heaven? I saw a nurse looking down at me. "Where am I?" She told me the name of the hospital. I realized I'd failed again. I still felt that way when the police officer who found me, dying in my car, came in and told me, "You're lucky." I'm sure he didn't feel very lucky after I let him know how much I disagreed with him. He couldn't get away from me fast enough.

That same policeman came back a few days later and when he found me a bit more calmed down he told me a story that just amazed me. He said he'd been patrolling the same area for 20 years. "In all those years," he said, "I'd never gone on that road where I found you. But the other night when I came to the turn-off I just knew I had to take it. I wasn't surprised when I saw your car. You were in bad shape, my friend. I didn't bother calling for an ambulance, just hauled you into the backseat of my car and brought you straight here. You might not think so but I'm telling you, you're lucky." When he told me that I started thinking that maybe God, whoever He was, didn't want me to die. Or maybe He didn't want me around either.

I felt safe in the hospital. Maybe it's because hospitals had been "home" for so much of the first ten years of my life. Maybe it was the confinement. I'd spent a lot of time enclosed within four walls. I began meeting with a psychiatrist, who was nothing like the one at Rubery Hill Asylum. He was quiet, seemed rather kind and was wise enough to know that I knew the system, the game, well enough that I wasn't going to let him get close to me. I'd decided no one would. Not again. Not ever.

After I got out I went back to coach-driving. My marriage to Pat had been annulled, since it wasn't legal to begin with. I saw my kids when I'd come to town between shifts on the road, and that's where I was spending more and more time. But there was time I couldn't account for, times when I wasn't on the road or with my kids. I wasn't losing my memory, really, but I'd realize that several days had passed and I had no idea where I'd been or what I'd done. I remembered everything else I was doing, but there were these "gaps." I think I probably went back to places where I'd been hurt. I was still searching the past, searching for answers. Why? Why had those things happened? In time I would find parts of answers.

Coach-driving once again provided me what it always had; safety. It was something I could do well, a way to bring people enjoyment, to make them happy without letting anyone really get near me at all. "I bet you're the life of the party, Tony!" I heard that from passengers all the time. I'd smile and laugh, and never tell them how wrong they were. I never *went* to any parties. I knew none of them would believe me if I told them that. They wouldn't believe it because I couldn't explain it. Even if I'd wanted to, I couldn't explain the darkness, the emptiness that was inside me. You can't explain that to someone who hasn't felt it. I'd become a cliché, I guess. I showed people the "me" they seemed to want to see, the jolly clown, always laughing and enjoying every minute of life. If they could have seen the truth, they would have seen the unhappiest person they'd ever known.

It wasn't just the total loneliness that hurt. I hurt physically too. I developed arthritis in my back and hips from the polio I'd had as a child. I sometimes had to take a lot of pain medicines just to get through the day. The thing is, I didn't care. I'd given up on the idea of suicide, even though some days I hurt terribly in every way. That's why the fog, the numbness from the medications suited me. There was no joy in life anyway. I dragged myself to work everyday and, at night, home to an apartment or to a hotel room on the road. And always, the nightmares.

I'd been living that way for more than ten years. Driving travelers around Europe for three weeks out of every four, being friendly with everyone and friends with no one. One day, on a trip to the south of France and Spain, another coach from the line I drove for had broken down. As I pulled my coach up the other driver yelled up, "Which way you goin'?"

"Back to Birmingham," I replied, and as I said it I wondered why I had. There was no reason for me to go to Birmingham. I no longer had a place there and Pat and the kids had moved on. But that's what I said.

I had only about 20 passengers on my 56-seat coach, so there was plenty of room for the people who had to get off the other coach. I'd been driving longer that day than the other driver had, so I let him get behind the wheel and I enjoyed visiting with some of the travelers on the trip back to England. The passengers who'd been on the other coach included two nice-looking young women, and I told myself I should demonstrate the coach line's friendliness and appreciation for the customers by paying special attention to them. They seemed to appreciate the attention as much as I did.

Denise

Their names were Dawn and Denise and they said they were sisters, twins even. I didn't believe they were twins and since I figured they were teasing me, I wondered whether they really were sisters. As we talked on the long drive back to London, I allowed myself to become convinced they were indeed twins, but obviously not identical twins. We had a nice chat, about nothing really.

When we arrived back in London and everyone had gotten off the coach, Denise came up to me and said, "I heard you tell the other driver you were going to Birmingham. Would you mind giving Dawn and me a lift? That's where we live." I said I'd be happy to give them a lift and off we went. It was an interesting ride and the best conversation I'd had in years. Denise, I quickly learned, hated men. Fair enough. I hated women. I wouldn't trust a woman as far as I could throw her. Denise wouldn't trust a man as far as she could see him. Dawn, who didn't have a strong opinion either way, was seated right between us and just seemed to be enjoying the conversation.

Oh, the horror stories we shared! Denise was recently divorced from a man who had turned out to be quite a prize. He wasn't at home much, but when he was he abused her, emotionally and physically. When he wasn't home he was out with other women. Small wonder she had a low opinion of men. I shared some, but not all of my history with Denise; enough to keep the game of "Men are all such pigs; no, women are much worse than men" even. It was great sport and when I dropped Denise and Dawn off in Birmingham I thought that was the last I would see or hear of either of them. Although I did find Denise intriguing. Man-hating and all, there was something different about her, not that it mattered; I'd never see her again.

A couple of weeks later, in Paris, another driver for the coach line gave me an envelope. "Here, a passenger asked me to give you this," he said. Inside was a postcard from Denise, along with a photograph she had taken of one of the scenic sites on her and Dawn's trip through France and Spain. Denise had written her telephone number on the postcard so, that night after we'd finished traveling for the day, I called her. She thanked me again for driving her and her sister home from London. She laughed when I told her how much I'd enjoyed our spirited conversation. Then I somehow got the courage to ask her if she would go out with me and, to my pleasant surprise, she said she would. A few weeks later, as the trip through Europe was winding up, I actually found myself looking forward to returning to England. It was the first time I'd felt that way in years.

I wanted to make a good impression, so rather than drive my own car, I hired a rental. Not a luxury car, but much nicer than my own. It isn't that I wanted Denise to think I was better off financially than I actually was (well, that was part of it), but I didn't want her to go through life hating men, because of one man. I didn't want her thinking that all men were just interested in what they could get from her, rather than what they could give her. I wanted her to "travel in style" for the short time we were going to spend together.

We traveled in style up to Blackpool, the popular seaside resort on the Irish Sea. We went to the theater, had a lovely dinner. We really had fun, and I felt something different inside me. Whether this was something that was really going to last, I just didn't know. I knew it was going to take time to find out. And I found myself looking forward to that.

We got to know each other over the months as we spent more and more (and *more*) time together. And I think for the first time I actually felt something I'd never felt before in my life. Something different. I think if we look at it closely, that new thing I was feeling was something called love. For years, since the end of my marriage, I'd had no time for women. Now I found myself wanting to spend all my time with *this* woman. I was well past 30, but I was behaving like a lovesick kid. When I looked into Denise's eyes, I melted. And so, we got engaged to be married.

Then we got un-engaged.

Then we got engaged again.

Then un-engaged, again.

I'm not sure how many times we went through that ritual. What I do know is that we kept feeling unsure, scared really. Neither of us wanted to make the same mistake again. Neither of us wanted to be hurt that badly again. What I knew more than anything is that I didn't want to hurt anybody, certainly not Denise. I felt like I'd rather die than hurt her. Finally we decided, we can do this. We can make this work. We *will* make this work. It was just that simple. Of course, this being me, it wasn't that simple at all.

It started when we went to the local government office to get a marriage license. We both filled out all the papers and turned them in, and a few days later we learned that my marriage to Pat had *not* been annulled. The paperwork to annul the marriage hadn't been properly processed so, as far as British law was concerned, I was still married. I couldn't believe it! First I couldn't be legally married to her, now I couldn't be legally unmarried?!

Denise and I had to get an attorney to submit a petition to the Crown Court to have my first marriage annulled before I could marry Denise, or else *I* would be a bigamist. What a mess! And it got worse. British law at that time allowed for the annulment of a marriage for only two causes; non-consummation of the marriage or bigamy. Since all this was documented in public records the local news media were free to look at our sordid little story, and some reporters decided it would make fascinating reading and soon I found myself being asked to talk about our ordeal. I said, "Sure, I'll talk to you." I was bitter.

But after talking to the press I started thinking a little more clearly, and I realized it wasn't just strangers who were going to read this. People who knew my kids were going to read about it too. And I knew who would be hurt the worst. So I called the reporters and told them I didn't want the story to run, and I told them why. And I told them I was withdrawing my permission to use the information. To my shock and relief, they pulled the stories from the editions of the papers that circulated in England. I was too late to get it pulled from the early editions, which went to Scotland, but the stories didn't run anyplace where my kids would have to deal with the fallout, and for that I'm eternally grateful.

If only it had been that easy to get the annulment taken care of. It took eight months for the court to receive the petition, send it to the proper offices where it could be processed, then make its way back to the court in Birmingham and finally back to us, informing us that my illegal first marriage had been legally set aside. And so after all that, Denise and I were married in the village of Daventry. I was 36 years old.

Things changed, but not fully. I was still looking for something. Even though I admired Denise, I didn't trust her. I had trusted Pat, and look what it got me. After that I told myself I would never trust anybody, and I wasn't ready to start, not yet. So I kept a lot of things to myself, and that made life very hard for Denise.

Not long after we were married we started our family. First Christopher was born, then Andrew just over a year later. I think I was probably afraid of getting too close, loving my boys too much, because I'd already "lost" two children. It was a selfish thing to do, trying to protect myself that way and even though it hurt Denise very much, the person it hurt the most was me. I robbed myself of the joy I could and should have had, if I'd allowed myself to really embrace my boys from the moments they were born.

Instead I was casually embracing a lot of activities. Some of them were quite worthwhile. Others were not. It was around this time that I started working with the medium I'd become acquainted with. I don't want to even think about how much evil that association would have brought into our home, if not for Denise and her genuine goodness keeping it out, maybe without even knowing she was doing it.

I can honestly say I was involved in more good things than bad, a lot more. We had a lot of ideas to organize and conduct something called workshops for the disabled, to create activities and really do things for disabled people. It was during this period of time that I actually got lost in doing good works, but for the wrong reason. All the good I was doing was just to cover up my own pain. I started up a number of Phab Clubs. Phab is a national charity in Britain; the acronym stands for physically handicapped, able-bodied. As the organization's mission statement says, the aim is to promote and encourage people with and without disabilities to come together on equal terms. Not hard to understand why that would appeal to a man who still clearly remembered how it felt to be the kid on crutches, the kid with braces on his legs, the kid with crooked feet. I was spending much of my waking hours doing whatever I could so that people who were hurting might hurt a little less. But I was ignoring my own pain; I was just covering it up, and that was hurting the people who should have mattered to me the most.

During this time I started doing something I'd never done before, except in passing, for brief moments many years apart. I started thinking fairly often about God, but still not trusting Him. I mean what was the point, really? What would God want with me? Who was I? Nobody. God wouldn't want me, I was sure of that. Denise had by then given her life to the Lord, and she'd done it consciously and deliberately. That was one more struggle we had. I seemed to have one foot in one camp, the occult, and one foot in another, being involved in activities and organizations that were really helping people. Denise on the other hand, was doing everything in her power to be solidly on the side of good all the time.

As we struggled on we seemed to never gain much ground, but I guess we were achieving a little something in life. The work I was doing paid just enough so that we could make a down payment on a house. Nearing 40, for the first time in my life my little family and I were living in a house that belonged to us, or would after we paid off the mortgage. I'd never known that feeling before, having my own home, and I liked it. Then real encouragement came into our lives.

I met a fellow who had a financial company and he asked me to come and work with him. This is it, I thought. This is going to be my breakthrough. So I got busy learning everything I could about mortgages and insurance. I worked very hard at it, putting in a lot of hours. I even scraped together some money to invest in the business. He and I agreed that I would be paid a commission on all the business I brought in and, as a minority part-owner, I would share in the firm's profits. I was so excited about what I was doing. The hard work, the long hours seemed like nothing. The time just flew by. And before long, we were ruined.

"It just didn't work out." That's what he told me when he closed the firm. I had no job. I hadn't been paid in months, which meant we were months behind on the mortgage on our home. And we lost it. The bailiffs came and took possession of the first house I'd ever owned, prior to selling it at auction to pay the mortgage. Denise and I and our two little boys were, quite literally, out on the street.

But in many respects that turned out to be a good thing. Just down the road was a small village, Lilbourne, where there was a vacant "council house." English towns and villages have houses that are owned by the local councils, and they're rented for very modest sums to people who can't otherwise afford a place to live. Now, Lilbourne was one of those places where families live in the same houses for generations. There hadn't been a vacant home there for years, but right at the time we lost our home a council house in this village came vacant. The Lilbourne council had heard about Denise and the boys and me when we got in contact with them and, within days of being put out of our home we had moved into a new home, in a place where we were surrounded by people who really cared about us. On the one hand we'd hit bottom; I had no job, we had two small boys, we were living in a home provided by the district council. But even though it was still hard, this was the point, the time, when I began to understand who I really was, when I could start getting well in every way, emotionally, mentally, spiritually and physically. And it was the start of Denise showing me what the love of Christ really was about. She stood beside me and actually walked me through some of the darkness that was so much of my life. When things began to get better again, I knew that this time they were *really* getting better, that there was no going back to the old, bad ways.

As Denise was helping me, I was helping other people. I had ended my involvement with the spiritualist. I never claimed to have her "gift." I knew I couldn't see the future or get messages from the dead or know about things that had happened to people in the past without being told. But I could discern the real meaning of what people were saying. It's a genuine gift, and one I think I've always had. People felt comfortable talking to me, even about things that were very uncomfortable for them. I was counseling with people through clubs and groups I was organizing and running. Slowly I began to realize, I really liked my life.

Then came the explosion.

An Admission of Guilt

I left the house to go to work one day, and to this day I don't know what happened. I never arrived there. I "lost" five entire days. I don't know where I went and no one I knew saw me during that time. Five days after leaving for work I was found wandering near an airport. I had no idea why I was there, nor any idea where "there" was. I was taken to a hospital and the staff contacted Denise, who came and took me home. A day or so later the police showed up at our door.

The groups and clubs I was running were all charitable, non-profit organizations. The money to operate them came from a number of sources, including some government funding. The books for one of the clubs showed money was missing, money that had come from the government. The police put that together with my five-day disappearance and me being found near an airport and came up with what was, to them, not just a logical conclusion, but the only possible conclusion. I'd been embezzling money and had tried to run off.

They took me to the police station for questioning, which was not pleasant at all.

"We know what you coach drivers are like," one of them said (I was still driving tour coaches part-time) "You've got a woman at every stop."

I just looked at him. "If I thought the way you do," I said quietly, "I wouldn't work at a police station. I'd work in a sewer." I wasn't making a joke. He didn't laugh. He didn't hit me either, although I thought for a moment he might.

The police didn't arrest me that day, and when they sent me home they told me I wasn't being charged, but I would be under investigation. After investigating the matter and me for eight months detectives found that no money was missing. This particular club had four different funding sources and four different bank accounts. I had paid some of the club's bills with money from a government-funded account, but that money wasn't supposed to be used for those bills. For practical purposes I'd committed the crime of not paying attention. For legal purposes, I'd misappropriated government funds. The police considered it a very minor thing, nothing more than a technicality, and they decided to just drop it.

Although I had been cleared by the police, I now had a very large cloud hanging over me as far as the government was concerned, and they weren't about to let me anywhere near federal grant money. Since many of the clubs and groups I was running got at least some of their funding from the government, I was finished in that arena. I went back to coach-driving full-time. I hated being away from Denise and the boys for a week or two at a time, but I had to make a living and this was something I could do. So I did, until the night I came home to find the police waiting at the house. They arrested me and told me I was being charged with theft for the matter of the misappropriated funds.

I felt like a murderer. The police took away my passport. I had to report to the police station three times a week. I couldn't work as a coach driver, because I couldn't leave the country. What could I do?

I was taken to the Magistrate's Court, charged with theft and was told the Magistrate's Court could take care of the matter without a trial. But I'd been charged with theft and I knew I hadn't stolen anything. For that matter, so did the police, and I wanted my name cleared publicly. So I asked to for a trial in the Crown Court. A trial date was set and we waited. Six months.

From time to time during that half-year the newspapers did stories on my case. I'd become somewhat well-known in the region as what we would now refer to as an advocate for the disabled. One time I traveled around England on a motorcycle that had a wheelchair fitted to it, to show that people with disabilities could enjoy the same sorts of things able-bodied people did. I raised a lot of money for programs for disabled people. I had been involved in a lot of good projects and had been the person who started more than a few of them. Maybe it was my way of trying to make up for all the things I'd done that weren't good during my younger life. I guess it made a great story; do-gooder accused of doing bad. The papers were fair for the most part, and reported everything that had happened and that no money had actually been taken, that I'd been careless, not dishonest, and that no one had gotten away with anything, nor had the government's money been spent on anything but activities for disabled people.

On the day of my trial a friend had loaned me her car to drive to court. "See you tonight," she said as I drove off. I smiled and waved but in the pit of my stomach I had a sick and certain feeling that I wouldn't be coming home that night.

When I got to court I learned that the charge had been changed, from theft to misappropriation. I had steadfastly pleaded not guilty to theft, but I felt I couldn't honestly ask the court to find me not guilty of the charge of misappropriating money. That's what I had done, no matter how innocently I'd done it. I pleaded guilty.

Timing, we're told, is everything and on that day in that court my timing couldn't have been worse. The case right before mine involved a man who was accused of stealing 250,000 pounds from the government. My case involved only a small fraction of that amount, but the judge was not in a lenient mood. Before he pronounced sentence he looked at me and said, "You've had your chance." He was talking about my past. He'd seen my criminal record, that I'd started appearing as a defendant in British courts when I was eleven years old. I was almost 40 now. I knew I didn't have any chance of avoiding prison. He sentenced me to six months. I don't know if this is a comment on human nature in general or just me, but my first thought was, "I've got my friend's car. How am I going to get her car back to her?" Maybe I was in shock. My attorney told me not to worry, that he'd get the car to my friend.

As I mentioned, when I came to court that day my attorney told me the charge had been changed, from theft to misappropriation. On hearing that, I changed my plea, from not guilty to guilty. But I believe there was more that he hadn't told me. I believe that there'd been some plea-bargaining going on that I didn't know about, and that in exchange for a reduced charge there was agreement among the attorneys and the judge that I would serve time in prison. I wouldn't have been so quick to plead guilty if I had known that was part of the deal. I didn't know about the deal at all. In my ignorance, or idealism or whatever, I assumed the charge had been changed to reflect what the police investigation had found. Obviously, I was wrong.

I was loaded onto a bus and taken to Winston Green Prison, an old Victorian-era prison in Birmingham. My heart sank as I was taken in through the double doors. For the first time in nearly 20 years I was locked down again. The routine hadn't changed at all. Brought into a small hallway, told to take all your clothes off, shown into an open shower room and watched by a guard as you wash, given a thin town to dry off, handed a stack of prison clothes, get dressed, then led to a cell and locked in. The thought that this is where I'd be for the next six months made me almost physically sick; especially since I knew there was nothing I could do to change anything. I worried about what people would think; our neighbors and those who'd been so kind to us. How would they treat Denise, I wondered.

Like our friend who loaned me her car, Denise expected me to come home after my day in court. She learned I'd been sent to prison when she talked with a friend who heard it on the radio. Later reporters were at our door, asking her how she felt about her husband being sent to prison for six months. As she closed the door she politely said, "Please, go away."

Two days later a miracle happened, in a sense. Very early in the morning a guard woke me and said, "Get dressed. You're being transferred." I was driven about 70 miles to a very different sort of prison in Leicestershire. From the outside it looked like a very secure place, which of course it was. But on the inside it didn't look like a prison at all. Instead of cells with bars, there were rooms. For my first two weeks there I was in a dormitory-style room with about 18 other men, while I waited for a private room to become available. That's how most of us were housed, in our own rooms. Each inmate had a key to his room. We were free to walk about the building and the grounds. This was like no prison I could have imagined.

I began studying theology, through a church that had a prison ministry. I thought that I wanted to become a minister. One of the prison staff told me that if I wanted to have special privileges to continue this course of study I would have to explain why I felt I was should have those privileges. What he didn't tell me is that I'd have to stand up in front of 250 prisoners and tell why. Well, I did. I told the assembled inmates that I felt I'd been called by God to be a minister. I told them that I'd made mistakes in my life and now I was asking for their blessing. I thought I'd get a rough time from them but, their reaction was totally the opposite. Many of them started seeking me out, asking me how things had changed for me, asking me to help them with the things that were hurting them.

So I was permitted to study for the ministry, but I wasn't a full-time student. It was still a prison, after all, and we prisoners had work to do. At this prison that included making shoes and I worked in the shoe factory. My job was to inspect the finished shoes to make sure the work was done properly. Not fascinating work perhaps, but it could have been much worse, as I well knew.

Although we had our own rooms, we weren't allowed to just do with them as we pleased. We were required to keep them clean and tidy and we had weekly inspections to make sure we were maintaining them properly. I was very fortunate in my room assignment. Whoever was in there before me took very good care of things. I talked with other prisoners who had to spend hours getting their rooms cleaned up so they could pass inspection by the guards.

On one inspection day it seemed the governor of the prison was paying more attention to me than he was to the condition of my room. Finally he said, "You don't remember me, do you?" I said I didn't.

"I was your house master when you was at Borstal," he said. "I never thought I'd ever see you back here. What happened? What have you been doing all this time?"

Once I got over the shock of being recognized by someone I didn't think would remember one kid nearly 20 years later, I told him. We talked, mostly I did, for quite a while. After I told him about the events that landed me back inside he said, "That's not right. Why don't you appeal?"

I told him that if I appealed I'd still have to serve my time while the courts considered my appeal, and there was no way to get back the time I'd already lost.

And I thought if my appeal was turned down I might lose even more time. "No," I said, "I'll do my time and get out." So that's what I did.

But I wasn't just marking time. I kept studying theology, and I became a sort of informal counselor to other prisoners. They trusted me. They knew I wasn't judging them. How could I? We were all in prison. And that discernment I had about people and what they were feeling, more than just what they were saying, helped me gain their trust as well.

Denise came and brought the boys to visit me a few times during the six months I was serving my sentence. It was wonderful for me and maybe surprising for her. She could see that while I was glad to see her and our children, I was "getting better" in ways I never had before. I was changing, probably without me even realizing it.

Two days before I was released from prison I was called to the Prison Governor's office and he read me the riot act. This was standard procedure for all prisoners prior to release. He wasn't just picking on me. He was quite stern, warning me about how bad it would be if I messed up again and wound up back in prison. But he and I both knew that wasn't going to happen. He could see that when I walked out of prison this time, I'd never walk back in as an inmate, that I'd never do anything that would put me back behind bars. He knew he didn't have to tell me the things he was saying. By law he did, but he knew I shouldn't have been there.

Two days later, at 7 a.m. I got up, showered and dressed in my own clothes for the first time in six months. I gave my room key to the guard and walked down the hall to the front of the prison. I walked outside. A guard opened the gate and I was released. Denise was standing there. We hugged like we'd never let go. She'd come for me in a broken-down little banger of a car. We got into it and drove away from the prison. I wondered whether the car would even make it back to our place, but it did. Barely.

We walked into our little house in Lilbourne. I was home. And I was scared. What was I going to do? Where was I going to go? I was afraid to even leave the house. What were people, our neighbors, going to think about me? It wasn't very long before I found out. No one ever said one word to me about my being in prison. All anyone ever said to me was, "We're so glad you're home," and "How can we help?"

I should have expected it. People I barely knew, people I didn't know at all, kids from our church, had taken the time to write to me during the six months I was locked up. The letters and notes and cards expressed so much kindness. "We're thinking about you," they'd write. "We're praying for you and for your family."

Finding Religion

I had to find a job, so I applied for the thing I'd always done. I still had my coach driver's license and after a couple of interviews I quickly hired on with a tour company. Soon I was back at the wheel, driving buses all over England and Europe. I hated being away from home so much, but what could I do? We needed an income. And the people of Lilbourne had work, of a sort, for me when I was home.

As I mentioned, there was never any condemnation or unkind words of any sort from anyone in the little village where we lived. No one ever pointed or whispered, "That's the man who was in prison," when we were out in public. And when people came around to our home it wasn't just to ask if we needed anything. Sometimes they asked for help in figuring out problems they were having. They'd read or heard about me counseling other inmates while I was in prison. Now they were giving me the opportunity to do the thing I loved best; helping other people.

But most of the time I was on the road. It was summertime and the coach lines were very busy with tours. In August, 1987, a strange thing happened. I had just returned from a tour of Europe when my boss called me into his office and said, "There's a Wesleyan group from America coming in. We want you to do their tour."

"You must be joking," I said.

"No, why?"

"I don't wanna spend two weeks drivin' them holy saints around."

"Well, it's your choice," he said, "If you won't drive 'em we'll get another driver to do it and you can get yourself another job."

So I found myself steering my bus to Heathrow Airport, to pick up a bunch of Wesleyan ministers from the United States. I wasn't at all happy about it. It might seem odd that someone who wanted to study for the ministry in prison was so strongly against being a tour guide for a group of ministers. But even though I was starting to understand that God had a role to play in my life, I guess I still had a foot in both camps. I still didn't want to give myself to Him. Surrendering felt too much like losing. However I also didn't want to lose my job.

One of the ministers was a man named Bob O'Dell. He was from the small town of Salamanca, in Upstate New York. Bob was the "bus captain" for the tour, which meant he got to sit up at the front of the bus whenever he wanted to. He and I hit it off right away; a good thing, since we were going to be around each other all the time for the next ten days. As we talked I just felt there was something important about him, although he wasn't at all self-important. He felt like a father. Even though we had just met, I felt like he was someone who was concerned, who really cared about me and what was going to happen to me. I felt like I could talk to him about anything. Part of that was me thinking, "I'm never gonna see him again anyway." Coach drivers are very good at that. But Bob was someone I *wanted* to talk to. I wanted him to know about me, and that wasn't like me at all.

And he was funny. One day we were traveling down the motorway and traffic was very heavy. It was a handful for me and all the other drivers on the road.

From the back Bob called out, "Tony, do you think you need to pray?"

"I might," I yelled back.

"Just don't close your eyes when you pray, OK?"

Bob was the kind of person you felt you knew well as soon as you met him. He was ready to be your friend right away. And he was very easy to talk to. I'd never told anyone about the abuse in the approved school, but I told him quite a bit about my past, my childhood. I told him where I'd come from and what I'd gone through, including what I had just gone through and how I was making it. Of course in that regard, I was and I wasn't. I was just trying to get back to normality. Looking back, I realize that Bob listened to me a lot more than he talked to me.

One day toward the end of the tour, Bob said, "Tony, I'd like you to talk about your life to some kids from New York City. I run a camp for kids at Salamanca, and I know they'd love to hear about your life." I thought, "Yeah, I can just see me doing that," but I just kept looking straight ahead and didn't say anything. I was "paying attention to my driving." Bob said, "Well, would you?" I said I'd think about it.

I dropped Bob and the other ministers off at the airport and figured that was the last I'd ever see or hear of any of them. I drove off and went home to Denise and the boys. A few days the phone rang. It was Bob. "Are you still considering coming to New York," he asked. He'd like me to be there in May of the following year. I heard myself saying, "Yeah, OK, I'll come." I had no idea how I was going to afford to travel to America in less than nine months. I had no extra money and I knew I wouldn't when the time came to leave. I figured when the date got closer I could tell Bob, "Sorry, turns out I just can't make it."

But we kept in touch through the Fall and Winter and into the following Spring. Bob was a mentor to me, like a father really, and the encouragement he gave me was just great. As May drew closer Bob said, "We need to set a date for your speech to the kids." We agreed on a date, but I knew I wouldn't be there. My plan hadn't changed. Closer to the time I was supposed to come I would say, "Bob, I'm so sorry. I just don't have the money for the trip." Then really strange things started happening.

I had changed jobs and was now working for National Express. It could be described as the United Kingdom's version of Greyhound. National Express coaches travel all over the country. One day I was up north, in a town called Bradford. I was driving the Bradford-to-London run. It was five in the morning. A little old lady came up to me and said, "Oh, driver. Can I get a ticket to London?" I sold her a ticket and didn't think anything about it. She got onto my bus and a few minutes later I closed the door and drove off for London. I'd forgotten all about her by the time I was pulling into the station at London. I was getting the passengers' suitcases out from under the bus when this same lady walked up and put something into my hand. I thanked her and put it into my pocket. It wasn't until later that I remembered her exact words. She said, "Driver, you will need this." Before making the return trip to Bradford I had a few minutes so I went to phone Denise. While I was on the phone I put my hand into my pocket and pulled out what the old woman had given me.

"Denise," I said, "You aren't gonna believe this."

"What?" she asked.

"Somebody just gave me a dollar bill. And it says 'In God We Trust.'"

"You're going, you know," Denise said.

"No. There's no way."

Two days later I got a tax refund check in the mail. It was for the exact amount of the airfare to New York.

When I went in to work I stopped by the boss's office and asked for time off so I could go to New York. He said no. Time off was assigned on the basis of seniority, and I hadn't been with the company very long. Well, I figured, that's that. I can't go.

Five days later the boss called me into his office. He told me one of the more senior drivers had left to take another job. "He was going to take the time that you wanted off. Do you still want it?" I was going to America, to New York.

And there's another strange part to this story. All the bus tickets have a return portion that passengers have to turn in. The old woman's return portion was never handed in. To this day I believe that passenger who appeared to me to be an old woman was in fact, an angel.

I had to leave Denise behind, and I was scared. I'd been on buses all over the UK and Europe, but I'd never been on an airplane flying to the other side of the world. I needn't have worried. The flight was actually quite pleasant. Getting through customs at Kennedy International Airport in New York City was not. It took two and a half hours, and I was on my feet the whole time. I was hurting, believe me.

A young man from the church in Salamanca was there to meet me when I came out of customs. "We didn't know if you were coming," he said. "I got really worried when it was taking so long." Me too.

The church had paid for my ticket to Buffalo, New York, and when I got there it was like a joyous reunion. Bob was so pleased to see me and we hugged for a very long time. We went to dinner with a number of people from Bob's church and others who were associated with the camp. They drove me all around the area and it was quite an exciting time. The next day I went to the camp and talked to the kids.

As I began to speak I looked into all those bright young faces, and I could see the hurt. At first I thought, "My God, they're just like me," but I very quickly forgot about my problems and what I had been feeling. All I could think about was how much I wanted them to not hurt. After I spoke they all thanked me. I didn't know what hearing a middle-aged man who talked funny, telling about my life, could do for them but they seemed so grateful, as though I'd done a really big favor for them.

On the last night I was there, we were invited to a big banquet, hosted by the Mayor of Salamanca. After we finished eating Bob told me, "They've got a special award for you." I'd been in enough public offices to notice the beautiful pen sets on the desks and I figured that's what I was going to get. I was thrilled. I didn't have a desk back in England, but I'd be sure to find some space on a table for my pen set.

The Mayor stood up to speak. First he introduced a local man who had worked for the State of New York for 30 years and the Mayor gave him a key to the City of Salamanca. Then he called for me to come up. He introduced me as "our guest from England, who has traveled so far to share his inspiring story with our young people." Then the Mayor presented *me* with the key to the City. Did they know what they were doing? Giving the key to the City to a crippled kid, a former criminal, a bus driver?! I was speechless. They gave me a lot of other souvenirs to take back to England as well. It was just so overwhelming, so memorable. Later that night I got to thinking about the future, *my* future. I started thinking about coming to America, and I knew that's what I was supposed to do.

At first my thought was to work with prisoners, the prison ministry I imagined when I was imprisoned for the misappropriation offense. But the more I thought about imprisonment and what it does, I began to think about the toll it takes on prisoners' families. When you're in prison you don't have to make a lot of decisions; most of them are made for you. Where to stay, what to wear, when to get up, what to do at every hour of the day, what to eat, when to go to bed; inmates don't have to give any of that any thought. It's all mandated. Even an inmate's choices of recreation are very limited. But how hard must life be for an inmate's family? How do the ones on the outside go about the necessary work of day to day living when there's this void, created because a member of the family is locked up? It seemed to me that no one was thinking about that.

When I got back to England I thought about it some more, and I felt that, yes, this is what God wants me to do. I knew I was a good counselor, and I don't say that boastfully. But I knew I had a gift for listening and helping people see the course that would help them if they'd follow it. Granted, I had much less of a gift for seeing the course *I* should follow to make my own life less difficult. But maybe that was changing.

Denise and I talked and prayed about it a lot and we both felt confirmed in the thought that what God wanted of us was to help people in the U.S., so we started looking into coming to America. But our plans were delayed by the sort of everyday catastrophe most of us just glance at in passing. And this one first nearly killed me, then left me almost as good as dead.

The Crash

I didn't know how much longer we would be living in England, but I decided that however long it was, I wasn't going to spend it being apart from Denise and the boys. My days as a coach driver were over. I found a job driving delivery trucks. It didn't take me to scenic places around the UK and Europe. I didn't meet people from all over the world. But every night I came home to the people who mattered more to me than anything else in life; Denise and Christopher and Andrew.

One day after I'd made the last of my deliveries, I got a call from the dispatcher to pick up another parcel. I found the business, picked up the package and started driving home. My route took me under a bridge not too far from where we lived. In the very large vehicle I was driving I'd have to drive down the middle of the narrow road under the bridge, taking up part of the driving lanes in both directions. I stopped to make sure there were no other vehicles coming toward me and, seeing it was clear I started to pull out.

As I did car traveling about 80 miles an hour came speeding toward me. I had no place to go, no way to avoid the collision. You hear how at such moments, your life flashes before you; mine did, an instant before the car slammed full-speed into the driver's side of the truck, and me.

I'm told it took more than 45 minutes for the police, the ambulance team and the fire brigades to get the wreck untangled enough to pull me out, load me into the ambulance and take me to the hospital. I was out cold for a short time. I should have been dead.

A few hours later at the hospital I honestly didn't feel that bad. To be sure, I was shook up and had pains in my back and my neck. But I wasn't in the kind of excruciating pain you'd expect for someone who had just been hit by a car going 80 miles an hour, and more than anything I wanted to go home. I hated hospitals! I'd spent more than enough time in hospitals when I was a kid and I was through with them. I told the doctors, the nurses, anyone who came by, that I wanted to go home...*now*. So, they put a stabilizing collar around my neck, took a lot of x-rays and couldn't really find anything that seemed serious enough that it might kill me, and they allowed Denise to take me home.

As we were coming in the door the telephone was ringing. Denise picked it up. A nurse was calling from the hospital. "Mrs. Sarjant," the nurse said, "Have your husband carefully lie down and make sure he stays still. We've got an ambulance on the way to your house."

"Why?" Denise asked, "What's wrong?"

"The doctors just finished taking a closer look at your husband's x-rays. He's broken his neck."

I had walked into the house when Denise brought me home and, as at the hospital, I didn't hurt too badly. But by the time the ambulance got me back to the hospital the shock had subsided and the pain was absolutely unbearable.

I had fractured a bone in the lower part of my neck. The doctors immobilized me completely, putting me in traction so my injuries couldn't do any further damage. As I lay there I could feel my legs going numb. I thought, "This is it. I'm going to be paralyzed." When I was sent home two weeks later the doctors told me, "Tony, you're not going to walk again. You're going to have to use a wheelchair for the rest of your life."

All I could do was lie in bed, so for the first week or so I spent my waking hours doing what I did best; feel sorry for myself. Then all of a sudden it hit me. I realized, "I've been through this once before, when I was a little kid. I came through it last time, I'll come through it this time. I will fight this." I knew I could just get out of bed and walk away from it. Not right away, but I *would* walk.

A lot of friends came to see me and we had our discussions right there in the bedroom. It was a good time, and also a time of searching, for myself. I got in touch with the local college and was told I could actually do course work from my bed. So I began formal study in psychology and counseling and I began to heal, in a number of ways. When you study psychology, you have to take a really serious, close look at yourself. And this time, I wasn't going to just condemn what I saw.

Over the next two years I went to college at home, and I got out of bed and walked. I couldn't really walk very far, but I could do little things. I could walk a few steps from the bed to the wheelchair. Our boys loved to push Dad around in the wheelchair and while I didn't like being in the chair, I loved seeing the joy in my children's faces as they helped me get around. Often Denise would push me in the chair and sometimes I'd get around by myself in the chair. But I always knew it wasn't permanent. I knew I would walk. I knew *I would make it!* I didn't know where that assurance was coming from, but I knew it was real.

Still, the battles came. The nightmares came back, horrible as ever. I was scared. Feelings of unworthiness came back upon me. Emotionally I'd push Denise and the boys away or I'd withdraw. I sometimes wondered if maybe I deserved what had happened. "Am I no good? Is this why I'm suffering?" But, no. Somewhere in the pit of all that, there was a spark of life, of hope. That hope is what I rode as I started going forward, started getting back.

I got back to getting around with crutches. I'd hated them when I was a kid, but now they were a sign of progress. Then I was able to put the crutches down because I could walk with a cane. It took me four years from the crash until I could walk with a cane. Physically and often emotionally it was hard, but really those were four *good* years. It was a time when I had to look at myself, honestly and fairly. It was a time when I had to analyze what had happened; what others had done to me; what I had done to myself. It was the time, really, when God started working in me in a very serious and lasting way.

I was asked if I would become the Area Director for the Reachout Trust, a Christian organization that works to help people who've been involved in the occult. I said I would because I knew the dangers, the darkness of it. It was something I could do from home and something that really could be the start of a walk again.

Two years later we moved back to Daventry. Because of my injuries, my disability, we had to move from Lilbourne, where the types of care and services I needed just weren't available. Our boys liked living in a bigger place with more kids. I was hurting still. I was starting to get my life back in my control but I still wanted to *run*. Mostly I was scared; scared of me. It's a horrible feeling, being scared of yourself; not knowing who you are or what you do. So I didn't want people getting close to me. I pushed Denise away, emotionally. I'd disappear for hours, or sometimes days. She came to the only conclusion she could; she thought I was having an affair. I still hadn't told her about the abuse I'd been subjected to when I was young. Here I was, 40 years on, still tortured by it; still having nightmares when I'd go to bed, and living a kind of nightmare, resisting the one thing that could, and eventually did heal me; love.

Denise showed me a love I'd never seen before. I don't know how she did it. I would have walked out on myself if I could have. I couldn't stand being around myself. But Denise stayed. She stood there. I tried pushing her away, but she wouldn't go. I loved my boys, but I was so afraid I'd hurt them. How could I be a good father, I wondered, when I didn't even know what a father did, what a father *was*? In time I knew I had to face it. I didn't want to, but I finally realized I had to. I mentioned the abuse to a doctor and he sent me to a counselor. On my second visit I walked in and the counselor said, "So then, tell me about the abuse and let's get it out of the way." With more strength than I knew I had, I turned his desk over and walked out.

Not long after that a good friend had made an appointment for me and Denise at a Christian counseling center called Fresh Fields. The day before we were scheduled to go, I ran. It was the only thing I knew how to do. I went back to the place where I'd been hurt. I'd done that before but this time it was different.

The approved school wasn't there anymore. It had been knocked down.

On the site where my life had been nearly destroyed a housing development had been built up. The homes were filled with families. And something in my spirit said, "Look, this is who you can be." I went home and Denise told me I couldn't keep running away. She also told me that if I wouldn't do what I needed to do to heal my spirit, she would take the boys and leave. She just couldn't keep being strong for both of us. She was worn out. I was still confused about a lot of things, but one thing I knew for certain was that I couldn't lose Denise. I told her I was ready to keep our appointment at Fresh Fields.

We were to have counseling together, but first we would each meet with counselors separately. At the start of my session the counselor offered a prayer, then I began talking about the abuse. After a few minutes something happened that I had never experienced in my adult life; I started to cry. Tears welled up in my eyes and streamed down my face. As they did I felt like something inside me had burst, and a lifetime of pain was rushing away from me. I was 52 years old and for the first time in my life, I could feel the hurt leaving me; I had the most beautiful feeling, beyond anything I could have imagined. I sobbed so hard I shook, and it felt good; it felt right. It was as if I was a baby, surrounded by love. I couldn't see His face, but I knew I was feeling God's love. I could feel His arms holding me. And I heard His voice saying, "Where have you been looking? I'm right here." I'd been looking in all the wrong places all my life. But He'd been there all the time. He'd been carrying me all those years.

Now it was as though there was an old pottery pitcher over my head, and as the water poured out it turned gold, and it washed over my head. And then I could finally tell the truth. There was no secret anymore. We all carry secrets, and sometimes those secrets can kill us. If we don't deal with them, those secrets can finish us in a lot of different ways.

We spent three days at Fresh Fields and had a number of counseling sessions and after each one I felt lighter and lighter. Within just a few weeks afterward people who'd known me for some time were saying, "Tony doesn't even seem like the same person." Of course, it wasn't just the counselors who were helping me. They were there to hold open the door to the *real* source of help, of healing. And that was God.

One day God said to me, "You've got to forgive."

I thought, "Now hold on there, Lord! Let's be fair here. How can I forgive someone who's done something so horrible to a child? And not just to me, but to who knows how many other children. I can't forgive that."

He said, "You have to forgive. I've forgiven you."

"Alright," I said, "I have to forgive. But how? How can I forgive that?" I just couldn't get past that.

He whispered in my ear, "Someone who would do that to a child is sick. You can forgive someone who's sick, can't you?"

And I knew I could. It was hard and it took a long time, but just saying the words, "I forgive the sick person who did that to me," over and over was the start of me being released from all that pain and suffering.

Denise's Perspective

Quite early on I noticed that Tony was always very secretive, not as though he was hiding something he'd done wrong, but there was something that had a very intense hold on him. He was terribly guarded about even the most unimportant things. He wouldn't speak out on anything, and I wondered why, when he was so outgoing in so many other ways. It wasn't until years into our marriage that I learned about the sexual abuse he'd suffered as a child. To this day he finds it hard to trust very many people, and when he and I met he didn't trust anyone. He now admits that he didn't even trust me for the first ten years of our marriage. I knew, or I thought I knew what a truly good man he was, but his inability to let me get close to him made it hard, even for a very positive person like me.

That positive attitude toward life is a gift. I don't know where it comes from (well, I do actually; it comes from God), but that gift is what kept both me and Tony going for a very long time. I might not have realized it consciously, but at some level I understood that I had to be healthy, emotionally, for both of us.

It was odd watching him relate to people other than me. Everyone thought he was the life of the party, and he was grand to be around in a group. He was always very clever and funny. From the first day we met he could make me laugh, but that's the only side of himself that he showed to others, so they never got a full appreciation for him. I'd think, "Oh, if only you could know the real Tony, you'd be ever more impressed with him." But the real Tony wouldn't show himself to anyone, not for a very long time.

I'm sure I saw him gradually begin to change, but it was very slow and I'd find myself being very impatient, not in anything I said to Tony, but certainly in my prayers. "Oh, God," I'd think, "why does this have to take so long?!" That's the side of me that I didn't let people see. I tell myself that if I'd known about the abuse years before I did, I might have been able to help Tony begin to heal sooner. But I didn't know. He wouldn't tell me, and the way things happened was just a process we both had to go through.

Even though Tony wouldn't let me or our boys be as close to him as we wanted to be, he was always in my thoughts and my prayers. We had two beautiful dogs, and the boys and I would take the dogs out for long walks. Those were my "prayer walks," for Tony. I can see now that my prayers were being answered, but it isn't as though Tony was the way he'd been for years, and then one day he was suddenly "well." It was so gradual that I only noticed the changes months or maybe years after they'd started happening. For example, Tony could never say he was sorry, about anything. Whenever we'd have a disagreement I'd be the one to say "sorry." After a while I started asking myself, "Why am I always the one saying I'm sorry, even when he should?" But I knew, sensed really, that I said "sorry" because I could and he couldn't. So I had to, and to end whatever unpleasant situation we were in I'd say "sorry" and we'd get on with things.

And then there was a change. Tony started saying he was sorry and I thought, "Wow!" He'd never said he was sorry to anyone in his life, and now he was doing it. It might seem like a small thing, but it was a very big change for him, and for us.

Another change was that he stopped "running away" when people dropped by the house to visit or even just to chat. Tony would leave the room. He wasn't rude about it; he'd excuse himself and whoever had come by would assume that Tony had something he had to do in another part of the house, but he just didn't want to be around other people in that way. Then after a time I noticed he'd stay in the room and visit. And before long people were dropping by to see Tony. It was while we were living in Lilbourne that he started counseling people. On the one hand it was wonderful to see him helping people, and he gave the most thoughtful advice and really did make a difference in people's lives, but on the other hand it frustrated me that he couldn't apply that advice to himself.

Part of my frustration was because I wanted Tony to really take all the good things he was advising people and apply it to me; to me and the boys. But the advice he was giving, good as it was, came from his head, not his heart. I knew Tony's heart. I knew the wonderful goodness that was in him, and I wanted him to share that with others, especially with Christopher and

Andrew and me. But he was still afraid to let anyone see what was in his heart, even himself. "Why can't you see what's in your heart, Tony?" I'd wonder.

Looking back, I can see that he started to see what was in his heart during the three days we spent at Fresh Fields, the Christian counseling center. That was our new beginning and it came after what was almost the end of us. When Tony took off for several days right after our friend had arranged for us to go to Fresh Fields, I thought, "I can't take this anymore." I told Tony that when he returned home. I told him if he wouldn't do anything to try and get better, I would take the boys and leave. I told him how much I loved him, and what a good man I knew he was, but if he wasn't going to see that, I couldn't stay with him. He saw that I meant it. A few days later we went to Fresh Fields.

The people who direct the counseling center describe the place as a Christian village, and they say it's been like that for 400 years. There is a peace about it that I can't describe, but the feeling I had as soon as we got there was the most marvelous I'd ever experienced. It was almost as if God had anointed this village as a place where people could come and be healed. The peace Tony felt there let him know that this was a place where he was safe and where he could do the things he needed to do to become the man I knew he was, the man I knew God wanted and needed him to be.

Time to Go to Work

Life was starting to get good, *really* good. I had gotten my diplomas in psychology and counseling and I began counseling work in earnest. At first I worked without pay, counseling people in our community who needed help, but who had no way to pay for it. I worked with families. I helped parents and children see that, by using the principles for living that Christ taught, they could overcome the challenges and the behavior problems that beset so many kids, kids who are hurting inside. I trained people to work with children and families, and helped set up "safe houses" for kids who had no place to go. I was doing the work God wanted me to do.

I hadn't wanted to do it. When I began studying to be a counselor I had the idea that I would work with adults in prison, or who had recently been released from prison. I had no interest in working with kids. Of course that's the old joke, isn't it. If you want to make God laugh, tell Him your plans. *His* plans for me were different from mine. It was as though He said, "That's where you're going, boy. You're going to work with these kids." And so I did.

I was past 50 when Denise and I realized that we had work to do somewhere else. It wasn't a decision that we had reached after discussion, but it was the most powerful feeling. We both knew we were supposed to go to America. We were doing research on the Internet and that's how we learned about a youth ministry in Tennessee. This seemed to us to be the right direction so we applied to join up with them. Then we waited, and waited, and waited. As it turned out, God had more work for us to do before we left England.

While we were waiting for some word from America the Lord touched us again. We felt we should help children through foster care, in particular by keeping children of the same family together, but I couldn't see how that idea was anything but madness.

I thought, "Well, Lord, I can't do this." I knew I loved children, but because of my background I couldn't imagine us being approved as foster parents. Still, we applied with the government and, to my surprise, we were accepted. What surprised me even more was how enthusiastically we were accepted. Here's the official social work assessment report on Denise and me:

> Tony and Denise have both presented as being highly motivated and committed in respect of their application. They have co-operated fully in completing homework/written assignments. During our discussions they have demonstrated insight and awareness of child care issues.
>
> Tony and Denise have excellent communication and social skills. They impress as being a mature couple, in the sense that they handle people and situations with insight, intuition and wisdom. An important focus of this assessment has inevitably been the impact of a large sibling group arriving in their home. Tony and Denise believe they are as prepared as they can be and are realistic about the challenges that lie ahead.
>
> In our opinion both Tony and Denise have a realistic and flexible approach to the adjustment they will need to make at such time as a sibling group is placed and will be able to work through the likely challenges caring for a sibling group will bring. As a couple they have the necessary reserves of energy which they will be able to draw on.
>
> Their warmth and sensitivity to the feelings and needs of others are apparent in addition to their ability to put people at ease. They are sociable people who very much enjoy family life as well as pursuing their own individual interests.
>
> Denise, although initially less extrovert than Tony, has a strength of

character and a sense of humour which become evident on closer acquaintance and her calm and unruffled approach instills confidence.

Tony has demonstrated considerable insight into the abuse which he experienced and the effects this had on him. He has made a remarkable recovery from these experiences, and whilst being aware of his ongoing vulnerability, he will be able to give much support to a child(ren) who has experienced a similar background.

Tony and Denise are a couple who have "survived" many painful and stressful experiences and in doing so they have demonstrated their resilience and their ability to continue to support each other through these. Both Tony and Denise have demonstrated their ability to show sensitivity to people who are vulnerable and in need of help. They have given a high level of support to members of their network who have gone through times of difficulty.

We believe that their relationship has been tested by the many trials and traumas they have faced and has enabled them to become closer and stronger as a couple.

Our opinion is that Tony and Denise are a couple whose personalities complement each other. Denise will provide the nurturing, routine and flexibility of approach which will be necessary. We believe Tony's strengths will be his patience, sensitivity and his ability to relate/listen to children who have experienced difficulties.

We are confident that both Denise and Tony would be able to request additional support from both their supervising social worker and their own networks, if this is required following the placement of children. Their ability to relate to children coupled with their relaxed manner will encourage children to approach them with confidence. Tony and Denise have the skills and abilities to be able to provide children with a safe, secure and nurturing home environment.

A few weeks later we got word that our first family group was on the way to our home; six kids. The oldest was a thirteen-year old girl, but very "young" for her age, and terribly withdrawn. Her eight-year old sister, on the other hand, was a lot "older" than any child that age should be. This little girl had taken on the role of mother to her younger brothers and her older sister. Getting her to let go of that responsibility was a challenge, but nothing like the challenge the two oldest boys presented.

They were ten and eleven years old and, like their younger sister, wise well beyond their years and not at all in a good way. Life had been very harsh with them and they adapted the way a lot of boys do. They were very street-wise. Around the house they spoke often and openly about "jacking" stuff, not knowing that I had been where they were when I was their age. When they learned that long before they were born I'd known that jacking was street-code for stealing, they stopped talking about it at home. But they didn't stop stealing every chance they got.

The family also included a five-year old boy and a two and-a-half year old boy. The youngest boy had been so neglected that he wasn't even walking yet, nor did he talk. From the time he was able to hold a bottle he was given a bottle of milk and left to lie in his crib all the time.

These kids were a family by blood, but really they were six very separate, isolated children. Other than the eight-year old girl's feelings of obligation which circumstances had forced on her, there was no sense of kinship among them at all. They all thought only of themselves and how quickly they could get away. The first time we sat them down for a meal together we wound up having to set up a table outside and feed them in the yard. They were totally unused to sitting down and eating in what we thought was a "normal" way. There was nothing normal about it for these poor kids.

We had actually gotten a glimmer of hope when they first were brought to our house to stay. They had been to the house to visit and they noticed that something was different this time. One of our dogs had died the night before and several of the kids saw that I was feeling down. "Why are you sad?" one of them asked me. So I told them about the death of one of our pets. They seemed genuinely touched. "Oh, we're so sorry," the younger girl said, "It's a good thing we still have another dog." It thrilled us to hear her say "we" have another dog. And her compassion gave us hope and encouragement that she and her siblings hadn't been treated so harshly that we wouldn't be able to help them.

And help them, we did. At first they just wanted to run away, and who could blame them. They didn't know Denise and me and our boys. We were just another bunch of strangers, in a long line. But within a couple of weeks a miracle happened; they became kids, just children concerned with the things kids have on their minds and in their hearts. Of course it didn't happen easily. One of the first things we did was to take them all out shopping for clothes, and that was a big mistake. We should have taken them one or two at a time because while we were trying to pick out things for the girls and the younger boys, the two older boys were trying to steal everything they could hide under their jackets. The shopping trip was *not* one of our early successes.

Sadly, we realized early on that we weren't going to be able to help the two older boys. They'd been turned so hard that they just weren't able to function in a family setting. The day I had to take away a knife the eleven-year old was holding at his five-year old brother's neck, I knew we'd have to send the ten and eleven-year old back to the authorities. It was a very sad day for Denise and me. Those two boys didn't show any emotion at all, and that was the saddest thing of all.

After about three weeks, the turmoil of six troubled children joining our family of four was pretty much settled and we got a phone call...from America. We'd been accepted for the ministry in Tennessee. My first thought was, "No, this isn't what God wants." The kids were just starting to feel like maybe we were alright; maybe our home could be *their* home for more than a few weeks or months. I didn't want to upset their lives again. But I realized as well that some of what I was feeling, some of what I didn't want to leave, was the comfort of our home. We were beginning what turned out to be, really, the best year of our lives in England. We had a really nice home; we loved what we were doing; I was well-regarded in my profession; our boys, Christopher and Andrew, were growing into fine young men and they liked everything about their lives. I wondered, "Am I being too materialistic?" Maybe I was. So we decided we'd better look into what we would have to do to go to America.

It was early in 2003 when we first visited the U.S. Embassy to begin the process of applying for visas. The Embassy staff person we talked with noticed that I'd been to the U.S. before and he asked me what sort of documentation I'd been granted then. I told him I'd come on a waiver. He reminded me that the waiver asked if I'd ever been in trouble with the law, and he asked me how I'd answered that question. "I put down 'no,'" I told him. He knew quite a lot about me and he asked me why I'd declared that I hadn't been in trouble with the law, when in fact I'd served six months in prison. I told him that, under English law, legal records are "spent" after seven years. Up to that point he'd been quite the inquisitor, but he'd actually heard about that part of the law and his attitude changed completely. He became quite nice, telling us, "I'll do everything I can to get you there."

On our second visit to the Embassy we were told, "You have to have a clean record for at least 15 years in order to apply for a visa to work in the U.S." Denise and I smiled. We were experiencing another miracle. It had been 16 years since my 1987 guilty plea for misappropriation of funds. If we'd applied when we first started feeling we should go to America, in 2000, we wouldn't have gotten anywhere. We felt now that the Lord had "stayed our hand" and made sure we didn't start the process until it could end in success. Still, I had to write a letter detailing all the legal trouble I'd had, starting with when I was a kid. I put down on paper what had happened and why, from my point of view. I guess it was an explanation of my life.

In the meantime we got on with our lives, turning all our attention to the four foster children who had become part of our family. We loved those kids! And they'd changed so. The younger girl had stopped feeling like she had to take care of her brothers and sister; she could just be a kid and enjoy it. The older girl, who'd had no confidence in herself at all, had learned what we saw right off, that she was a bright child with a delightfully attractive way about her. Shortly after the younger girl turned nine she came to us and said, "I'm giving my life to the Lord." The five-year boy, who'd taken to stealing, following his older brothers' example, had quickly stopped taking things that weren't his. The little one soon started walking, then talking, then trying to be as grown-up as the others. Before long he was laughing and having the time of his little life in playgroups with other toddlers. We took them everywhere, and we kept the promise we made to them when they came to live with us; we gave them back their childhoods. We helped them be kids. And best of all, they became a real family, with real love and concern for each other.

Before leaving the house for my third visit to the Embassy I told Denise, "If God wants us to do this, we'll get a five-year visa. We can't do this work in America in under five years." She agreed, but we were both nervous that we might not be approved to work in the U.S. for five years. I sat down with the man who'd been working with us and asked, "Are our visas approved?"

"You don't have visas," he said. My heart sank.

"You've got permanent residency." Green cards!

For a moment I was numb. Then I started grinning the biggest smile of my life. I knew it was God's will.

I had very mixed feelings on the drive home. We were getting what we wanted, what we knew God wanted. But we would have to leave our foster children, and we'd have to tell them we were leaving.

They'd been with us for nearly a year, and were scheduled to leave our home in a few months, but looking into the faces of these kids we'd come to love so, and telling them we'd have to say good-bye sooner than planned, it nearly broke our hearts. We all cried, and hugged, and just held onto one another for a long time.

But we weren't going to just turn them back over to the system. While we were waiting for word from the U.S. Embassy I'd started doing some investigating to see if there was another couple who would take these four kids into their home as a family. We were confident that these were good people and that they'd provide a loving home for the children. Still, the day we drove the kids to their new foster home was one of the hardest days of our lives. But this part of the story also has a happy ending. We kept in contact with those four kids, and they just continued to blossom. Against terrible odds they're doing great, growing up to become fine young people. And they know that they'll always have each other.

The house was very quiet when we got back home. When we walked in Christopher and Andrew came into the living room and put their arms around us. They didn't say anything. They didn't have to. Our boys had loved those kids as much as we had. They played with them, took them to football (soccer) matches, watched out for them. Bringing foster kids into a home where there are already children can be a challenge, and it doesn't always work out. But it couldn't have worked any better in our home, and Denise and I will always be grateful to our sons for that.

Now we faced another challenge. Denise and I were moving to America. Our sons were young men with lives of their own; Christopher was 18 and Andrew was 17. We really wanted them to come with us. Andrew was all for it. Christopher most certainly was not. "I'm not going," he said. "I'm not leaving England." He made it clear this was not a matter for discussion. He was an assistant manager at the place where he worked, so he'd have no trouble providing for himself. I set about looking for a place where he could live. I wasn't happy about it and I kept trying to talk to Christopher about this subject he didn't want to discuss. I didn't want to break up our family. The four of us were really close. We had, in our family, what I'd always wanted and now it was going to end. One day when Christopher was home from work to have lunch, he and I were standing in the kitchen and I said, "Just try it for a year, son. Please. If you don't like it you can come back to England and I won't try to talk you out of it." He said, a little sharply, "Dad, don't put any pressure on me, alright. I'm coming."

I'd walked out of the kitchen before I realized what my son had just told me. I was nearly out of breath when I went back in and asked him, "What did you say?"

"I'm coming with you," he said. I didn't say anything. We just held each other and cried.

Everything came together. I'd been making plans for three of us to sail to America, now I had to scramble and see if I could find cabin space for four on very short notice. I thought there'd be no chance, that we'd have to travel in two groups. But on my first call to the shipping line they told me, yes, they had two cabins, very close on the same deck and, yes, we could have them. We were going to America as a family.

The day before we left there was a big surprise party for us. My mother had organized it and I was truly amazed how many people came. Only then did I realize how many people's lives we'd been involved in and what they really thought of us. People we hadn't seen in quite some time came. Over and over people told us how we had touched their lives. We thought we hadn't really done anything. We'd just been there, it seemed to us; if someone needed help and we were there, we helped. We didn't go out of our way looking for people to help. It just seemed that sometimes opportunities to help came to us and when they did, we helped.

The next day, September 14, 2003, my mother and stepfather drove us to the docks at Southampton. She and I still weren't at all close, but I guess we'd reached a sort of truce in our relationship.

I don't know if the momentousness of the occasion really hit any of the four of us. We were leaving the country where we were all born and the only place we'd ever lived, sailing half-way around the world to start a new life, really. And I don't think any of us felt any fear or sadness, just excitement.

Now, I know that as Christians we aren't supposed to seek for signs. We call ourselves people of faith, after all. But I haven't always been as good at it as I might be and one thing I'd always said was, "Lord, you're gonna have to send a brass band if you want me to go to America." There were about eight ships sailing from Southampton that day, some crossing the Atlantic, some down to Africa, others to cruise the Mediterranean, and as our ship pulled away from the dock, a band formed up on the quay and started to play; a brass band. We'd had tears rolling down our faces, but now we had to laugh too. And that's how we started across the Atlantic.

That wasn't the last time we had reason to smile on our voyage to America. One day at sea Denise and I were walking around the deck and she said, "You know, I'd really like to see some whales. Do you think we will?" We glanced over the railing and at that moment a pod of five whales swam past the ship.

For more than a week it was like that; just a fantastic trip. We had time, together as a family and privately as individuals, to reflect on the past and to anticipate the future. And all the way across the Atlantic, for eight days, we never had a wave over four feet high. It was as though an angel was treading the waters before us.

America

September 21, 2003 was a Sunday; the start of a new week for millions of people across America. For us it was the start of a new life.

We stood on the deck of the ship as we sailed into New York Harbor. So many feelings as we sailed past the Statue of Liberty, past Ellis Island. I thought about all the millions and millions of people who'd gotten off ships at Ellis Island on their way to becoming Americans. They must have felt all things we did. They must have been afraid, as we were. And they must have been excited too. We certainly were.

The ship docked and, immigration papers in hand, we made our way to the immigrations area. We proudly handed the Immigration Officer the documents we'd been given at the U.S. Embassy in England. He looked them over, then told us to sit off to one side of the room, while he went off to see someone else about our paperwork. I can't describe the feeling I had, as we sat there while everyone else, all the other passengers, walked past us and on to America. It was the feeling I'd had many times before when I was being detained. I felt like I must have done something wrong. I'm sure that was left over from my youth and all the times I *had* done something wrong. People walked by, looked at the four of us sitting there, and I kept feeling guilty, but don't ask me "of what?"

About 20 minutes later the Immigration Officer came back with our papers.

He said, "We don't normally get people coming in this way anymore. We aren't sure what to do, so I've got to go make a couple of phone calls." Then he left again. A few minutes later he returned and told us, "We're going to let you into the country for today, but you've got to go down to the Federal Building tomorrow."

We caught a taxi and went to the hotel where we'd booked a room before leaving England. I worried that we might not have any time for the boys to go sightseeing the next day and I wondered whether the next day was going to be our *last* day in America. I must say, this wasn't how I imagined our arrival in America would be.

Monday morning we got into a taxi outside our hotel and went off to the Federal Building, not knowing what they'd tell us after we got there. The Immigrations Officer at the docks had given us a card to turn in at the Federal Building and I handed it over to the staff person in the Immigration and Naturalization Service office. He looked at the card and said, "What do you want?" I told him that the Officer at the docks had told me to give him this card, so I did. He said, "Oh, well, I'm sorry. We've started processing you." I went and sat down next to Denise. "It looks like we're gonna be here all day," I said.

But we weren't. Not fifteen minutes later the staff man came back. "Mr. and Mrs. Sarjant, Christopher, Andrew? Here are your cards."

What a feeling! We were now, really living in America, legally. We were officially part of the American system. I couldn't really grasp what had happened, not fully. It was something I never thought could happen, certainly not to someone with a background like mine. This was the kind of thing that happened only in fantasies, only in your mind. But it was real. We practically danced out of the Federal Building. Then we went everywhere!

We went to the top of the Empire State Building; we went to Rockefeller Center, to Wall Street, to Chinatown, to the Brooklyn Bridge, to Central Park. The next night we went to a Broadway show, "Forty-Second Street." It was a wonderful way to wind up our time in New York City.

Wednesday morning our adventure continued as we caught a taxi to Penn Station. We didn't know then that it's the busiest railroad station in America, or that we were four of the 600,000 people who catch trains there everyday, we just knew it was great. Everywhere we looked we saw something new and exciting.

We boarded the sleeper car that would carry us to Atlanta, Georgia, the next stop on our journey. The four of us probably looked like flesh-and-blood clichés, with our noses pressed up against the windows as the Amtrak "Crescent" train rolled along, down through New Jersey, Pennsylvania, Delaware, Maryland, Washington, DC, Virginia, and North and South Carolina, before angling across the top of Georgia and into Atlanta. We marveled at the changing scene of enormous cities, small towns and open space.

When we woke up the next morning we marveled at the sight of the Amtrak station in Atlanta, but not in the way we'd thought we would. We knew Atlanta was one of America's biggest cities, the self-proclaimed "Capital of the South," and we expected to look out and see a massive station along the lines of Penn Station. We were wrong. We were *so* wrong. Atlanta's train station was, to be kind, small. Very small. So small we thought we must not have gotten to Atlanta yet. But we had. This was it. Time to get off the train, gather our things and find a taxi to take us to the rental car office. Things went better there. A very nice lady at the counter quickly found our reservation and after I signed the rental papers she handed us the keys to our car, directed us to the parking lot and we were off for the two-hour drive to Chattanooga, Tennessee, where we would be living and working.

Denise and I had accepted the position of house parents at Bethel Bible Village in the suburb of Hixson, Tennessee, north of Chattanooga. This children's shelter had been founded nearly 50 years before we went to work there. The place has the look of a farm, which some of the campus was before it was donated to the ministry. The children, mostly from five to eighteen years old, live in the seven cottages on the campus. The organization's mission is simple, "To provide professional programs, support services, and ministries to children and youth of families shattered by crime and troubled environments." And it's successful. The organization's research shows that 85% of the children who pass through its programs grow up to be adults in stable families, who don't abuse drugs and don't wind up on public assistance.

We were assigned to a cottage housing six girls who were in the process of transitioning out of Bethel Bible Village. They were sixteen to eighteen years old and all were attending the local high school or community college. Our job was to help them learn the independent living skills they would need as adults in the wider world. It was a lot like the foster care we provided for children in England. We found we enjoyed the work, to a certain extent. But after a few months I was feeling uneasy, wondering if this was what we were really supposed to be doing. I know now that much of my unease was because of my own background. Having spent time in institutions as a kid I could never feel totally at peace with any sort of institutional setting, even one run by an organization that worked so hard and so well to create a home-style atmosphere. But whatever the reason for it, I was having my doubts. I thought that maybe we needed to return to England. I thought about that a lot. I thought about it so much that at one point I was ready to go back. I later realized that I wanted to go back to a comfort zone, and that just happened to be England.

Denise was the voice of reason, as usual. She kept reminding me that we needed to pray so we'd know what the Lord wanted us to do, rather than just thinking about what we (or I) wanted. Fortunately she was listening for an answer to our prayers. One morning she said, "Tony, I feel that the Lord's told me something. He hasn't brought us all the way here just so we could give up and go back to England. We've only been here six months." She was right, of course. But I just couldn't shake the feeling that being house parents in Tennessee wasn't the work the Lord had for us to do long-term. I shared that with Denise and she said the sensible thing. "Let's pray about it." We did, and we both got the same confirmation. We *were* to stay in America. It's where the Lord wanted us to do His work. But He needed us somewhere else. We didn't know where, but with the faith that He would tell us, we gave our notice that we would be resigning our position. It was early Spring, 2004.

We moved into the apartment we'd rented for Christopher and Andrew (yes, it was a bit crowded) and started looking for work. Soon we had an offer of work in Knoxville, Tennessee. We would be full-time foster parents, caring for children in a real home setting, rather than in a big group arrangement. My own experience told me that a big place sometimes isn't the right place for kids who are hurting to begin getting better. It's too easy for kids in that setting to become a just a number or a last name. Too often there's nothing really personal about the care the kids get. So the job in Knoxville had a lot of appeal, and we were leaning strongly toward accepting it. Still, we kept looking.

Our job search brought us to the attention of the people heading a program that was just starting up in Billings, Montana. It was to be called T.E.A.M. Mentoring. The letters stood for "Teach, Encourage, Assist and Model" a Christ-centered life. It would be (and is today) a ministry directed toward people who are in jail or prison, those who've just been released from custody, and the children of parents who are incarcerated. I was approached about a position as Director of the youth program. I hadn't really had any formal experience in putting a program together from scratch. In England I'd developed and fine-tuned existing programs, but this would be very different. I couldn't see myself creating something out of nothing. Besides, we'd never heard of Billings and we had only a vague idea of where Montana was. Denise didn't want to move "Out West," and I couldn't see any reason to try and talk her into it.

Then we got a call from Denise's sister, Dawn. She and her husband Mike had gotten married in Jackson, Wyoming, eight years earlier and they were coming over from England to celebrate their anniversary in Jackson. Since we were already in America they invited us to join them. Well, we could take the time since we weren't working, so we said, "Yeah, we'll see you in Wyoming." Then we got some maps to see where Jackson, Wyoming, was exactly, and how you get there from Chattanooga.

We learned that Jackson, Wyoming, was about 2,000 miles from Chattanooga, Tennessee, and you get there by driving non-stop for two straight days. At least that's how we did it. Jackson is in a place called Jackson Hole. It's an enormous valley with spectacular high mountains on three sides and two National Parks to the north. The mountains known as the Grand Tetons, reaching to more than 13,000 feet, create the western boundary of Jackson Hole and the sight of them, at any hour of the day, is breathtaking as they stretch more than a mile above the valley floor. But even more than the natural beauty, wonderful as that was, we felt something very special there. We truly felt close to God.

Our time with Dawn and Mike in Jackson Hole was a treasure, and much too brief. After a few days we were in the car, leaving the Grand Tetons and the

Rocky Mountains behind as we drove back to our home, in the shadow of the lovely but much lower Applachians and the Great Smoky Mountains.

We had a lot of time to talk during our drive home, and we talked a lot about where we had just been. Looking over the map we saw that Billings, Montana, wasn't terribly far from Jackson Hole. Denise said, "Do you think Montana is like Jackson?"

"It might be," I answered.

"Maybe that T.E.A.M. Mentoring position is still open," she said.

"I don't know that they'd want me if it is."

"You won't know 'til you try, will you?"

"Right," I said, "I'll call when we get back to Tennessee."

The position was still open, and the T.E.A.M. Mentoring people were still interested in talking to me. When could I come to Billings for an interview, they wondered. We arranged an appointment. Two weeks after our trip to Jackson we were back in the car, heading west again, this time to Billings, Montana. We drove into a city of about 100,000 along the banks of the Yellowstone River, in a valley ringed by sandstone cliffs the local people call The Rimrocks. All the trees were beginning to sprout their leaves, and the whole center of the town was starting to turn green. It was lovely.

The interview was an interesting session. They asked me a lot of questions about me, about my life, about what I thought kids who were hurting needed most. "Love," I told them. "And someone who just wants to be their friend. Someone who doesn't expect them to be anything but a kid."

They talked to me about their plans, what they expected to accomplish in the first six months, twelve months, two years, five years. They were starting with a blank page in their plans to help the kids. It sounded like something I'd like to try. We shook hands and they told me they'd call me. When Denise and I got back to Chattanooga there was a message from Montana. T.E.A.M. Mentoring wanted me to design and run their children's program. We'd need to be in Billings in three weeks.

I was excited for only a few minutes before I thought about our sons. We'd brought Christopher and Andrew from their home in England. Christopher hadn't wanted to come. I'd pleaded with him to come so our family could stay together. Now Denise and I were leaving and we knew the boys, young men now, wouldn't want to move again only half a year after we'd come to America. I dreaded telling them.

As it turned out I needn't have worried. They were perfectly happy to stay in Chattanooga; something about girls. Andrew joked about our impending departure, telling people, "Mom and Dad brought us to Tennessee and now they're going to leave us here." Everyone laughed.

But the day we left I felt like I'd done just what my son was joking about. I'd taken my boys from their home, brought them to a foreign country half a world away, where they didn't know anyone, and now I was taking their mother and we were leaving them alone. It was heartbreaking. The night before Denise and I left we all went out for what should have been a nice dinner. The food was fine, but we were all crying. The next night two of us drove west again. I could hardly see the road through my tears. I think making that two-thousand mile drive for the third time in little more than a month might have been some sort of penance for leaving the boys. That's a joke. I think.

But I'm not rationalizing when I say I know now that our move from Tennessee was the best thing we could have done for our sons. Christopher was 20 and Andrew was 19 when we left. For the first time in their lives they were really on their own and it was just fine. They'd been making lives for themselves during the six months Denise and I worked and lived at Bethel Bible Village and after we moved to Montana they very quickly learned that they didn't need the "safety net" of Mom and Dad being just 20 minutes away. They learned, much sooner than they would have if we'd stayed in Tennessee, just how strong and capable they were. As their parents we couldn't have felt any more joy in seeing the men they'd become. If anything, the move brought us all closer as a family. Our sons learned that their parents' love didn't decrease with distance. I think they somehow felt our concern for them more deeply than they had when we all lived in the same place. I know they felt and appreciated the confidence we had, and continue to have, in their judgment and abilities as adults.

Seeing Clearly

Once we got to Billings and started working I began learning about myself. In the same ways that our sons were learning about themselves, I soon learned just how much I knew, even though much of it was knowledge I'd never told anyone or even consciously thought about. I had to take my ideas, my feelings really, and use them as the basis for a program that would reach children of imprisoned parents, in a way that those kids would feel safe enough to trust the adults who were trying to help them. Kids in those circumstances hear that all the time. They soon learn not to believe the people who say it because they don't ever see things getting any better. I prayed, as hard as I ever had, that I wasn't going to be just another adult who failed those kids.

Here are the most vital parts of the youth mentoring program I developed for T.E.A.M. Mentoring, along with Executive Director Larry Gaalswyk, which I believe God inspired us to see.

Keys to Success

Time Investment

Mentoring is a slow process. It does not try to get a lot done in small bursts or in a short amount of time. Like all healthy relationships, mentoring involves frequent contact and long-term commitments from both the mentor and the youth.

Commitment

Children at risk feel like failures and resist forming relationships. They will probably try to undermine the relationship with you. Remember that you should view your commitment as long-term investment, a commitment not linked to the child's first response.

Accepting your child as he or she is

*Actions speak louder than words. It is critical that the child understands that nothing he/she does will cause you to reject them...**nothing!** Be prepared to have the child test you on this. If, however, a child refuses to meet or says that they want to discontinue the relationship, respect this and consult with your (team) captain or director.*

Empathy

It is important to be an effective listener. Empathy means "to identify with and experience the feelings or thoughts of another person." Empathy requires us to hear feelings, not just the words, of a troubled child.

Trust

Trust builds slowly over time.

Sincerity

Be yourself. Don't try to be perfect...you're not. Remember what these children are looking for—someone who accepts them unconditionally and values them as worthy. If your culture is different from theirs, pay special attention to cultural cues and learn as much as you can about their heritage.

We created the program to function as a team so everyone involved, kids and adults, would understand that they aren't alone. To that end we drew up a contract that spells out what the mentors need to do, and to give them direction in doing it. It looks like this:

Children's Mentoring Team Players

Brief description of position:

A person on a team of two or more mentors who is committed to a "friendship with a purpose" with a child struggling from the consequences of having a parent who is incarcerated.

Benefits:

Personal growth in Jesus. The blessings are equivalent to ministering directly to the Lord. (See Matt. 25-31-46) Often the greatest blessing and growth is to the Mentors.

Major responsibilities/tasks:

Spend time with (youth) in leisure time activities: trip to a zoo, fishing, mini-golf, ball games, picnic, church activities, etc. In concert with others on the team, maintain weekly contact with your youth.

Qualifications:

Pastoral recommendation: All mentors must have written recommendation from their pastor, as the program is part of the church's outreach.

Certification: At least one mentor on a team needs to be certified by TEAM. Certification is given upon successful completion of 10 hours of training.

Character: Each mentor must agree to the policies and Statement of Faith of TEAM Mentoring, Inc.

TEAM Player: Each mentor will be able to work cooperatively and effectively with other mentors, be responsible and accountable to those in authority.

Criminal background check: Each mentor and his family members in contact with the (youth) must submit to a background check. This is required for the protection of all parties involved in the mentoring relationship.

Desire to share life and ability to spend time with (youth).

Supervisor:

Pastor, other 'TEAM Players,' T.E.A.M. Mentoring Director and/or Caseworker.

Investment Commitment:

time commitment minimum of two hours per week for at least 12 months

We also gave the mentors some counsel and suggestions for things they could do to help create a relationship with the children they mentor. It's based on finding common ground.

Creating Shared Experiences

It may be difficult to start a relationship with someone who has little in common with you and who comes from a completely different culture. However, with a sensitive approach it can be a rich experience for both of you. One way to get over these barriers and build understanding is by learning from each other and creating shared experiences with your (youth). Suggest culturally-related experiences, visiting museums and other places of cultural interest. The activities need not be expensive but should reflect the child's interests. Your interests and hobbies may influence the child also.

Ideas for activities to do together:

Church activities
Go see a movie
Swimming
See a ball game
Picnic
Mini-golf
Museums
Homework
The zoo
Go out to dinner
Skiing
Fishing

We worked very hard to help the mentors see what they were really doing. In that regard the program carries this counsel.

Effective mentors

Effective mentors are long-term investors. They commit to making deposits of unconditional love and Acceptance regardless of how unlovable a child may be. Remember that mentoring is a long-term commitment; the seeds you sow may not be recognizable for years.

* * *

I realized something very important as I worked with these kids and the adults I was training to work with them. I might have been doing a disservice to the kids we'd been with in Tennessee. The curse of the abuse and neglect I had suffered as a kid was sometimes both a blessing and a curse. I think there were times when I projected my own feelings, based on my experiences, onto the kids I was trying to help. Many times I did know what a child was feeling, but sometimes I didn't; rather I thought the child was feeling what I had felt when I'd been in that situation all those years ago.

That's when I understood what I needed to do, and why God had brought us to America. I needed to multiply my efforts, to multiply myself in a way, by showing other people how to reach, understand, and help kids. It's what I did, for the first time really, when I developed the youth program at T.E.A.M. mentoring. And it starts with the point I'd made so strongly in my interview when I applied to work in Billings. We have to love the kids. We have to accept them for who they are, right now. Not who we think they can be, or who we want them to be.

I can see that we can make more of a difference in the lives of children who are hurting and we need to. I know what can happen when people who know, or are willing to learn how to care for children and really love them, *don't* come into the life of a hurting child. I know because I've been that child…now I'm learning how to be that adult. I spent some 40-odd years of my life in hell, because of the hurt I felt, the secret I carried; the secret of the abuse. I look back on all the terribly destructive things I did to try and compensate, and to keep those secrets buried. The crime, the drinking, the occult, the suicide attempts; worst of all, pushing away the people who really cared and who really loved me in spite of myself, Denise and our sons. And I know that it all could have been avoided, if real love had come into my life when I was still a child.

It's said people learn best by example, and I know that's true. I've seen it in the lives of children who've begun to heal because of the loving example of people who truly care about them. I've seen it in a nine-year old boy who'd told his mother that he wanted to grow up to be like her, an inmate in the state prison. That was right before both the mother and the boy enrolled in T.E.A.M. Mentoring programs. Two months later, while he visited her in prison, they talked about what they were doing. She told him how she was learning, for the first time, how she could do the things she needed to do in order to stay away from drugs and crime. He told her about all the things he was doing, and the people he was meeting and the new friends he was making. He told her how he was doing really well in school. That rather shocked her. "Do you like school now?" she asked. "Oh, yeah," he said, "And I'm gonna go to college, Mom." After she swallowed the huge lump that was in her throat she asked, "You don't wanna be in prison?" Her son looked at her for a moment, then very quietly, but strongly he said, "No, Mom, and when you get out I know you're never gonna come back here either."

I know the power of learning by example because I've been healed by the loving example of Denise, whose love is a manifestation of the love God has for all His children. I've been healed in so many ways. Twice the doctors said I wouldn't walk; once when I was a very small child and again after my road accident. In both cases they later said I'd walk, but only with crutches. For years I had physical pain so bad sometimes I could hardly breathe, and I was told the best I would ever do is manage the pain with medications. Today, in my late 50s as I write this, I walk without crutches, without a cane and without a limp. I haven't taken pain tablets in years. That pain has stopped.

The deeper pain is almost gone as well. People who hear my story often say, "Oh, you're doing so well!" Well, yes I am, but I have to work very hard at remembering that because I know where I've come from. I know what I went through. But I really know that, finally, I love myself. I love my family. I love the Lord. And I love the children, of all ages, that I have the opportunity to help.

Finally, the most powerful example in my life is the one the Lord set. His divine act of atonement, taking upon Himself all the sins committed by all the people who've ever lived, and who ever will, so we can repent of those sins is so much more than I can begin to understand. And not just our sins, but also He took to Himself all the pain, physical and emotional, felt by all of God's children in all ages. He did that so we could bear things that would crush us otherwise, things that do crush some of us, the ones who never get help from others. And that, finally, is what I know He wants me to do. That's how I'm to "feed His sheep."

I'm able to help people begin to find their way because I think they know that I understand the darkness that envelops so many hurting people. How can you explain darkness to someone who's never been there. When a child says, "I feel empty," what does that mean? I know what it means. I know how it feels to be empty; to have nothing, no one. I know how it feels to have just yourself to help you survive. I remember all that. But the difference now is that void isn't there anymore. I feel like I'm a complete person. It took a long time getting there, but I feel now that I'm in a position where I can *really* help others.

One night when Denise and I were serving as house parents we were sitting in the living room with a young girl who looked so terribly sad. I could see she was hurting, so I got up and walked over and knelt down in front of her. I felt as much love for this young child as I'd ever felt for anyone. I wished I could take away her pain. Very quietly I said, "It's hard isn't it? When you're feeling torn inside, when you feel like two people, and you don't know which one is really you." She looked at me with a very surprised look on her face. "How did you know?" she said. I smiled and said, "I've been there."

The End

Man of Honor

Man of honor
You had your tough times
You've come smiling through
I know it wasn't easy
The pain and the misery
God's love saw you through
Man of honor he loves you
Time to honor
All you been through
I love the child in you
If I didn't know you
Swear you were an angel
Hand in hand God brought you through
Man of honor God loves you
Many highways
You had to follow
Standing for what's upright and true
If I didn't know you
Swear you were a hero
There are not enough medals for men like you
Man of honor I'm proud of you

By Denise Sarjant

Angels

You have always cared.
You are always there.
You two have always put
other people first, and I
am lucky enough to have
been one of those people you
have helped.
You mean more to me than
my own aunties and uncles do.
You two have been like my
angels and I thank God for that.
You will never know how much
you have touched my life.
So my Angels be safe and
good luck.

by Nicole, 15 years old
Given to us just before we left England to come to America.